114

Stewart River, on the following day. (41)
The weather is pleasant & warm & in the woods
numerous birds are chirping their merry tunes.
There were two birds in particular, whose notes
attracted my attention.
The one could be heard regularly every day at 5 a.m.
& again at 9 in the evening. Here is an exact reproduction of his merry tune —
He would keep that up for an hour at a time.
The other one sang during the day, in this fashion —
very punctuated.
There was a certain bird, called the camp-robber, that
would sneak around the camp & eat anything in sight.
The hawks devour these birds, whenever opportunity
affords. Frequently we hear the pitiful cries of these
camp-robbers, as they flit from tree to tree, with
a hawk in close pursuit. Pretty soon their
cries die out & we know that the hawk has again
demonstrated his superior strength and ferocity, & is perhaps
at that moment tearing to pieces the more tender
body of his fleeing victim.

WILLIAM SHAPE'S JOURNAL,
MAY 31, 1898

Faith of Fools

Faith of Fools

A JOURNAL OF THE KLONDIKE GOLD RUSH

WILLIAM SHAPE

Foreword by Frank Norris
Introduction by Lee Laney

Washington State University Press
Pullman, Washington

Washington State University Press, P.O. Box 645910, Pullman, WA 99164-5910

Phone 800-354-7360; FAX 509-335-8568

© 1998 by the Board of Regents of Washington State University

All rights reserved

First printing 1998

Library of Congress Cataloging-in-Publication Data

Shape, William, 1867-1960.
    Faith of fools : a journal of the Klondike Gold Rush / William
Shape : introduction by Lee Laney : foreword by Frank Norris.
        p.   cm.
    ISBN 0-87422-160-9 (acid-free paper)
    1. Klondike River Valley (Yukon)—Gold discoveries. 2. Klondike
River Valley (Yukon)—Gold discoveries—Pictorial works.
3. Klondike River Valley (Yukon)—Description and travel. 4. Shape,
William, 1867-1960—Diaries. 5. Pioneers—Yukon Territory—Klondike River Valley—
Diaries. I. Title.
F1095.K5S48 1998
971.9'1—dc21   97-47780
[B]   CIP

Contents

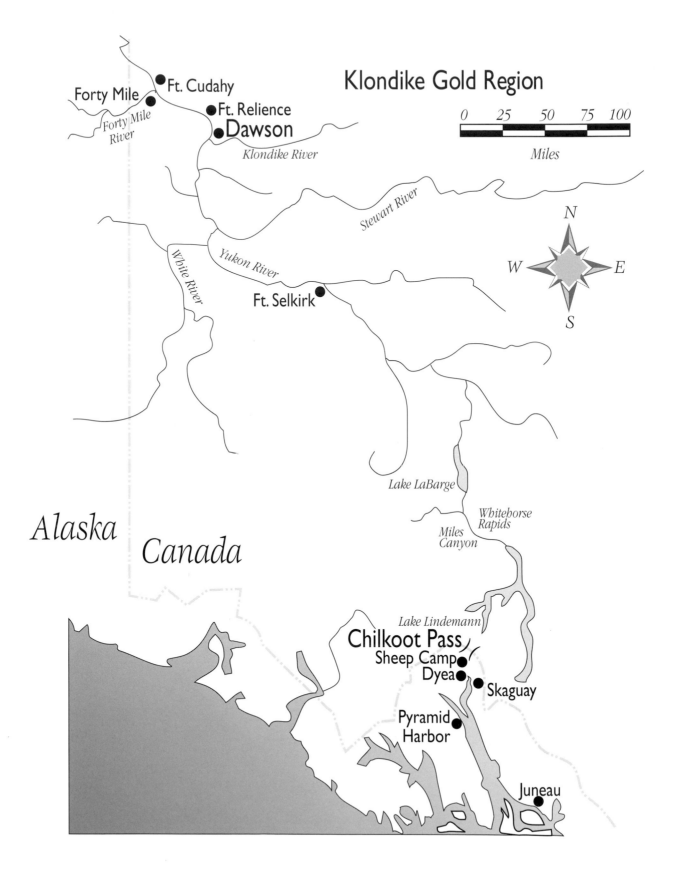

Klondike Gold Region

Forty Mile

Ft. Cudahy

Forty Mile River

Ft. Relience

Dawson

Klondike River

Stewart River

White River

Yukon River

Ft. Selkirk

0   25   50   75   100

Miles

N
W   E
S

Alaska

Canada

Lake LaBarge

Whitehorse Rapids

Miles Canyon

Lake Lindemann

Chilkoot Pass

Sheep Camp

Dyea

Skaguay

Pyramid Harbor

Juneau

Foreword

GOLD. ELEMENT NUMBER 79 on the chemist's periodic table, gold is a heavy, malleable metal that can be found in its free state either as dust or nuggets, or embedded in quartz lodes. Gold is a remarkable mineral, but its most remarkable quality is what it does to people. For thousands of years, in cultures around the world, gold has been coveted, valued, cherished. It was gold, for instance, that drove Cortez and Pizarro to conquer the Aztec and Inca civilizations; it was gold that drove tens of thousands of Forty-niners to California's mother lode; it was gold—or the lack of it—that drove William Jennings Bryan to cry out that "you shall not crucify mankind upon a cross of gold"; and it was gold that caused more than 100,000 adventurers from around the world, including William Shape and his companions, to leave home and family and strike out for the Klondike in 1897 and 1898. Perhaps Robert Service, the "Bard of the Klondike," put it best when he wrote:

> *Gold! We leapt from our benches,*
> *Gold! We sprang from our stools,*
> *Gold! We wheeled in the furrow,*
> *Fired with the faith of fools,*
> *Fearless, unfound, unfitted,*
> *Far from the night and the cold,*
> *Heard we the clarion summons,*
> *Followed the master-lure—Gold!*

The Klondike, important though it may have been, was only one of a series of gold discoveries that was played out over a forty-year period on the northern landscape. John Marshall's find, on a crisp January morning in 1848, started it all, bringing about the gold rush to California's famed Mother Lode. That remarkable discovery brought more than 100,000 argonauts to California during the next five years. Some mined the mountain creeks and others moved to the cities, but thousands more fanned out across the West looking for new gold strikes.

Many headed north. By 1858, gold had been discovered along the Fraser River in southern British Columbia, and shortly afterward came a far bigger strike several hundred miles to the north, starting the Cariboo rush. Then, in the mid-1870s, prospectors found gold in the big Cassiar region of northwestern British Columbia. The easiest way to reach the new gold fields was by way of Wrangell, in the new American colony of Alaska. The outwash of that rush eventually headed back downriver, and disappointed gold-seekers moved into southeastern Alaska.

Before long, Alaska had its first gold boom. In the summer of 1880, Joe Juneau and Richard Harris (on the advice of a Tlingit chief) found glittering flakes along Gold Creek. The Juneau camp soon became home to more than a hundred miners. In 1881 came another big discovery just across the channel at Douglas, and for the next sixty years, mining dominated the area's economy.

Miners, ever hungry for new areas to prospect, soon began to cast their eyes toward the vast Yukon basin on the far side of the Coast Mountains. The Tlingits had held an iron grip over the passes to the interior for hundreds of years, but the miners, using the U.S. Navy as a go-between, persuaded the Tlingits to become packers and guides for the gold-seeking prospectors. Under that arrangement, the first white prospectors crossed Chilkoot Pass in the spring of 1880. By the mid-1880s, several hundred each year made the trek, and as time went on the gold rush tide searched ever farther into the Yukon basin. In 1886, Robert Franklin discovered coarse gold on a tributary of the Fortymile River. The resulting Fortymile rush brought more stampeders north, and a new discovery on Birch Creek started the Circle City rush of 1894-95.

By the mid-1890s, more than 2,000 prospectors were working the tributaries and bars of the Yukon basin, and three of them—Skookum Jim, Tagish Charlie, and George Carmack—discovered gold along Rabbit Creek, a tributary of the Klondike River, on August 16, 1896. Following an old miner's custom, they told everyone they saw about their discovery, and within weeks the entire length of the Rabbit Creek drainage had been staked from one end to the other. News of the strike soon spread up and down the Yukon River, virtually emptying

out Fortymile, Circle City, and other camps, and many of those lucky enough to get in on the ground floor got rich. But communication with the outside world was notoriously unreliable, and few outsiders had any reliable information about the strike until the following summer.

Word about the new gold strike reached the outside world quickly, loudly, and dramatically. On July 14, 1897, the S.S. *Excelsior* arrived at the San Francisco docks. On board were the usual agglomeration of disheveled, hard-bitten miners. But word soon spread that these miners carried more than a **ton** of solid gold from the Yukon River basin. By the time the passengers were off the boat they were being mobbed and treated like conquering heroes.

The scene was even more chaotic in Seattle, where the steamer *Portland* arrived on the morning of July 17. The local *Post-Intelligencer*, having been appraised of its impending arrival, had an extra on the street that morning, announcing that the prospectors had "more than a ton of solid gold aboard...." The phrase "a ton of gold" would echo around the world, but it was, in fact, an understatement, because after the sixty-eight men came down the gangplank and weighed their loot, they found that the ship had actually carried more than **two** tons of gold. Based on that news, tens of thousands flocked to Seattle, causing one New York reporter to exclaim that "Seattle has gone stark, staring mad on gold." The frenzy continued for weeks, and Seattle's hotels, restaurants, supply houses, and shipping lines enjoyed a land-office business.

News of the gold find could not have taken place at a more propitious time. West coast cities, and the rest of the United States for that matter, had been going through tough times since the Panic of 1893; for most people, the "Gay Nineties" were less than enjoyable. Moreover, Americans at the time were particularly frustrated because the country, for the first time, had no new frontiers; the 1890 census, in fact, had confirmed that obvious fact. So the Klondike discovery gave Americans a desperately needed outlet both for those seeking economic gain and those who quested for adventure.

Everybody, it seemed, wanted to go to the Klondike, but few knew where the gold fields were or how to get there. Based on that ignorance, chambers of commerce and enterprising ship captains convinced hundreds of luckless stampeders to take untested, patently illogical routes. Those who knew the country understood that there really was no easy way to reach the gold fields, but three routes predominated over the others. The easiest, though also the most expensive, simply retraced the route taken by the *Excelsior* and the *Portland*; it took the gold-seekers to the mouth of the Yukon River, and then up the river to Dawson City. The route was so long, however, that almost no one who took it arrived in Dawson City before the Yukon rivers froze that October.

The other routes took the stampeders up the Inside Passage. At its northern end lay two trails over the Coast Mountains. The beauty of them was that they provided relatively short routes between the Pacific Ocean and the headwaters of the Yukon River system. All the stampeder had to do was hike over the mountains and sail down to Dawson City. It all seemed so simple.

But it was not. One trip over the passes was not too difficult—a stampeder could do it in three or four days—but each person had to carry more than a thousand pounds of goods, enough to live for a year. To do that, the stampeder had to go over the same trail ten, twenty, or even thirty times. In order to lighten the load and reduce the number of trips needed, some stampeders pulled sleds, some pulled carts, and a fortunate few used horses or dogs. Most, however, hoisted their goods on their backs and walked the entire distance. Add to this difficulty the fact that most of the stampeders hiked over the trail during the wintertime, when temperatures often dropped below zero and when the passes received thirty to forty feet of snow, and one can imagine the degree of difficulty the stampeders endured. Embarking on such a trip was not for the weak of heart, and the trip proved so challenging that more than half of those who left the West Coast port cities never reached Dawson City.

The White Pass Trail began in Skagway, a town that was nothing more than a homestead before the gold rush. The trail's backers advertised that the trail, forty miles between tidewater and Lake Bennett, was superior because White Pass was 600 feet lower than the nearby Chilkoot Pass. Those who used it, however, found that the trail was a partly constructed, rough-hewn path through the woods. Men and women, as a result, suffered to an extreme, and some

3,000 horses died along the infamous "Dead Horse Trail" during the first two months of the rush.

The alternate choice was the Chilkoot Trail, just a few miles west of the White Pass Trail. The Chilkoot began in Dyea and ended at Lake Bennett, thirty-three miles away. The trail, for many, was miserable from start to finish but the Chilkoot, unlike its rival, had been a Tlingit pathway for hundreds of years. Because the trail turned out to be so popular, it hosted a series of camps and towns every few miles along the route. Dyea, where the trail began, wound a mile and a half up the valley, and five other camps sprang up on the south side of the pass. All were temporary; they lasted less than two years. But in that brief time span, some grew quite large. Canyon City, half way between Dyea and the summit of Chilkoot Pass, housed a floating population of 1,500 during the spring of 1898. Sheep Camp, just below timberline, once numbered between 6,000 and 8,000 souls; it had more than sixty businesses, most of them either hotels, restaurants, or taverns.

The most difficult part of the trail was the ascent from Sheep Camp to the top of Chilkoot Pass. A three-mile climb from Sheep Camp brought the stampeder to The Scales; from here, the half-mile trek to the top was a trip never to be forgotten. Harley Tuck, who crossed the pass in April 1898, was so inspired by the scene that he wrote, "When about a mile from the summit we came into full view of it, and I just halted and gazed, for it surely is the sight of a lifetime." But Julius Price, who spoke on a more practical level, wrote that "it is about as fatiguing a climb as could well be imagined. Without exaggeration I should say the angle must be about 45 degrees." And yet another stampeder spoke for many when he jotted in his journal that "many lose their gold fever here and return home. The grade is so steep that one's pack bumps the one ahead when we walk close together."

Once stampeders reached the summit of Chilkoot Pass, it was a long, slow downhill grade to the Canadian lakes. During the winter and spring of 1898, Lake Lindeman and Lake Bennett were vast tent cities that held the stampeders until the ice broke. And because there was no transportation network organized to take the masses downriver, the chief occupation at the lakes was boat construction. The task was by no means easy, but somehow the inexperienced stampeders built more than 7,000 boats, dinghies, scows, and rafts that winter. Miraculously, most of those vessels made it all the way to Dawson. When the lake ice broke in late May, a vast armada headed downriver, everyone hoping to get to the gold fields just a little ahead of everyone else. When they arrived, however, they discovered what Dawson's residents had known for months—that the streets were not paved with gold and that, indeed, there was no easy gold for the taking.

A strong majority of the stampeders—perhaps 90 percent of them—used either the Chilkoot Trail, the White Pass Trail, or the Yukon River route. But a number followed less-traveled routes. One such path was the Chilkat Trail, which commenced at Haines

Mission, just a few miles from Skagway and Dyea. The Chilkat Trail, a traditional Native route, required more than a 200-mile land traverse over the Coast Mountains; for that reason, it was unattractive to most stampeders. The trail's backers, however, promised low passes, smooth grades, and other advantages to those driving beasts of burden northbound.

William Shape and his companions were in many ways indistinguishable from the rest of the Klondike tide. They headed north shortly after the *Portland's* arrival heralded the news of the great strike; they prepared for the trip in ways similar to others on the northward trek; and sadly, they were as unsuccessful at locating gold as the vast majority of their compatriots.

But Shape's trip (and his account of it) deserve special mention because, in other ways, his trip was a significant departure from the ordinary. First, Shape and his companions dared to take oxen along with them, and because of that choice, they initially headed up the little-used Chilkat Trail, which promised easy grades and available pasture. That their trek up the Chilkat River valley was ultimately unsuccessful is understandable considering the late season and the trail's treacherous footing; based on those circumstances, their interactions with the local Chilkats were less than harmonious. That experience, however, did not prevent his party from returning south over the Chilkat Trail, and his record of that traverse is one of the few known manuscripts detailing conditions along that little-used route.

Another remarkable aspect of Shape's narrative is the light he sheds on several of the more well-known events in the gold rush drama. By luck or circumstance, he stumbled across such famed incidents as the Sheep Camp whipping and the Palm Sunday snowslide, providing new insight to each. He also provides a fresh perspective on the other large and small ordeals that thousands had to overcome during the great northern trek.

A delightful complement to Shape's account are his photographs. The Klondike was an event that took place after photography had become fairly widespread, and historians feel fortunate indeed that a gritty corps of commercial photographers headed off to record pertinent aspects of the rush. Less common are snapshots of the rush taken by individuals, and the publication of Shape's many high-quality photos are a welcome addition to the gold rush compendium.

Finally, Shape's account deserves attention because of the level of detail and objectivity he provides for the entire trail experience. Shape was no saint. He was, however, a well-educated, persevering individual. A century later, readers cannot help but be surprised—and amazed—that anyone undergoing such physical and mental duress, week after week, would have had the ability to write more than a few random scribbles. But even under the most trying of circumstances he shows an impressive, dispassionate, arm's-length ability to separate important information from the ordinary and mundane.

Frank Norris
Anchorage, Alaska

DOC ROBEY, M. OPPENHEIMER,
COLONEL WILSON, AND WILLIAM
SHAPE IN DYEA.

Introduction

William Shape, 1867-1960
By Lee Laney

MY FIRST CONTACT WITH the Shape family occurred at a flea market near my home in Chico, California. Bill Shape and his wife, Eunice, were retired. For a little extra income and activity, they set up a booth most weekends. I could count on their booth for inexpensive toys to amuse my kids while I looked for more serious "game."

One rainy Saturday I noticed a box of faded photos on their table. As I looked them over, Bill and Eunice explained they were snapshots taken by Bill's grandfather on his trip to the Klondike gold fields in 1897-98. Priced individually, no single image was striking. Bill explained that he also had, at home, his grandfather's journal of the trip. The numbers on each of the photos corresponded to entries in the journal.

I quickly realized that the photos were invaluable as a set, especially with the accompanying text. I made an offer for the entire collection, and later that day picked up the diary and associated ephemera at the Shape home.

With a life-long interest in the history of photography, I've collected images for over twenty-five years. However, when I read the diary, my excitement over the acquisition of the photos was quickly eclipsed. Immediately, I was convinced the entire collection could be an important contribution to the history of the Klondike Gold Rush.

Some of the experts I contacted initially did not share my enthusiasm. However, perseverance is one attribute that has served me well over the years. More than ten years later, my enthusiasm has been rewarded with the publication of this book.

Experts do not always appreciate the "work" of amateur collectors in discovering items of historical interest. True, some collectors may hoard items that should be available for others to examine, evaluate, or admire. As amateurs, collectors may inadvertently damage or disperse artifacts that, intact, may provide irreplaceable information.

I believe we collectors fill a valuable role in the preservation of our past. Thousands of passionate amateurs are in the front lines in the retrieval, collection, and preservation of artifacts in many fields. Collectors are often the first to recognize the importance of artifacts, long before institutions and academics. My fellow collectors often divert from dispersion or annihilation items judged trivial by individuals or families as they "clean house." Such was the case with William Shape's diary of his trip to the Klondike gold fields.

For most people alive a hundred years ago, little remains beyond a headstone, a few photo portraits, and a name in the family Bible. Typically, recorded history carries forward the details of the lives of those people popularly believed to be important. Traditionally, oral history carried on the greatest amount of information. In today's culture, this rapidly fades. Even in those instances where great care is taken to preserve family artifacts, the mobile and unpredictable nature of twentieth century life often results in the destruction or dispersion of these things. Go to any second hand store or flea market and you will find scores of anonymous photos now disconnected from their context.

Occasionally, we are fortunate to have the written records of those individuals not studied by historians. Most typically, this is in the form of correspondence. Less frequently, it is in the form of a diary. These documents often provide the only first-hand account of events experienced by ordinary people.

With his diary of the year spent pursuing gold in the Klondike, William Shape left an intimate account of his experiences in an adventure shared by thousands. Several of these also chronicled their experiences in diaries or correspondence. A few, generally professionals, recorded the events photographically. William Shape's account is one of only a handful known to combine a personal written record with photos taken by the author.

We are fortunate that William Shape chose to record his trip this way. His intention was to share this with his family and friends back home. A hundred years later, it now reaches a much wider audience. In a unique way, it brings to life a pivotal era in the history of Alaska and the Yukon Territory, and one of the last human stampedes in search of mineral riches in North America.

In addition to the events of the Klondike Gold Rush, this account also gives us some insight into William Shape as a person. Simply by his choice of what he recorded, we have a glimpse of his personality. The fact that he undertook this adventure tells us much. However, what of the other ninety-one years of his existence?

❦

William Herman Shape, known as "Will" to his family, was born into a middle-class immigrant family in La Crosse, Wisconsin, on March 1, 1867. The fourth of eight children, Will had four brothers and three sisters. His father, Gustav Herman Shape, was an extraordinary person, and must have been a profound influence upon Will.

Gustav Shape and his wife, Gertrude, were both born in Germany. Gertrude came to the United States as an infant with her parents, the first white settlers in Richfield, Wisconsin. Gustav immigrated alone to New York at the age of seventeen in 1851. Around 1857 he moved to Milwaukee and acquired skills in telegraphy and bookkeeping, telegraphy being an important part of any business office prior to the availability of the telephone. In 1871, Gustav went to work for the Phillip Best Brewery (later to become Pabst) in Milwaukee. In 1877 he formed a partnership with Christian Voechting to bottle beer for the Joseph Schlitz Brewery—the first commercially successful beer bottling venture in the United States. When Charles Uhlien joined the company it incorporated, and eventually became part of the Joseph Schlitz Brewing Company, of which Gustav was a stockholder. At his death in 1885, his holdings were worth $200,000.

Beyond his business success, Gustav Shape had an active interest in music, which he imparted to his children. In addition to playing guitar and singing, Gustav played viola in the family string quartet, with Will playing cello. Gustav's other skills included fluency in five languages.

By the time Will was in his teens, the Shape family had become wealthy. This prosperity was reflected in their home in Milwaukee at 25th and Cedar, which included a carriage house and coachman. On at least two occasions, Will traveled to Europe with his father, both times first class. In 1883 Will and his father traveled alone. In 1885 his father took Will, then eighteen, with his older sister Emily (twenty-four), and three younger brothers, Adelbert (six), Herman (nine), and Robert (thirteen). The rest of the family, including Charles (twenty-one), Louisa (fourteen), and Oscar (four), later joined them for an extended stay in Switzerland.

One goal of this 1885 trip was to find a suitable apprenticeship for Will to learn the goldsmithing trade. This would indicate that, in spite of their wealth and artistic involvement, the Shapes valued the acquisition of a trade. Apparently, Gustav did not expect his son to be dependent upon the family's wealth, or to follow his footsteps in the business world.

Will recorded a detailed account of the 1885 European trip in another diary in pos-

session of the Shape family. Perhaps owing to his youth, he began keeping daily details, but this faded to occasional notes after the first month. When compared to his Klondike journal of thirteen years later, there are some interesting similarities. Superficially, his

WILLIAM SHAPE AS A YOUNG MAN. *COURTESY DOUGLAS SHAPE.*

literacy skills and penmanship are most apparent. This would indicate a formal education, completed when he was young. Family lore held that all the Shape children were educated in Europe. Will was also fluent in German.

Beyond the superficial details, Will's 1885 diary indicates he was a keen observer of his surroundings, physical and human. He compares the cities and peoples to his own home. He compares the demeanor of the captain on this trip with his earlier Trans Atlantic voyage. He also includes occasional drawings of interesting features. Of particular interest is his recording of much technical detail, including the exact speed of their train, a complete list of all towns passed between Chicago and New York, and the specifications of the steamer which took them to Europe. A bizarre twist is his account of the technical details of the Italian oven that cremated his father's remains after he passed away in Zurich.

Will did apprentice to a goldsmith in Zurich. He started working at the firm of Boshardt and Giorgi on November 19, 1885. Gustav's death at the age of fifty-two, in November 1886, must have been a blow to this family that enjoyed so many activities together. The rest of the family returned to Milwaukee shortly after the death, and Will followed in May, 1887.

Although it is not recorded in his diary, it is likely that Will met his wife, Louisa Schallenberger, during his stay in Zurich. A native of Zurich, her family was also wealthy. Louisa was born in 1871, one of four sisters. Will and Louisa were married in Ashland, Wisconsin, on March 22, 1890.

Their first son, Clarence, was born November 11, 1891, in Chicago. Their other son, Wallace, was also born in Chicago, on September 11, 1895. At some point before 1897, Will and his family moved to New York City.

While Will was gone to the Klondike during 1897 and 1898, Louisa and the children were quite comfortable. Clarence spent the year with his maternal grandmother in Milwaukee, while Louisa took Wallace to stay with her family in Zurich.

Upon Will's return, the family settled again in New York, on 116th Street near 7th Avenue. Will worked in the jewelry district as a watchmaker and jewelry repairman, until securing a position as manager of the Lion Brewing Company.

The Shapes apparently lived a comfortable life and encouraged musical talents in their children. For his tenth birthday, Clarence received a piano from his parents.

During 1901-02, Will was again traveling, but we do not know where. Louisa again stayed in Zurich, this time with both sons. The family then settled into a spacious apartment on Manhattan Avenue, at 111th Street, across from Morningside Park in New York City. Will and Louisa remained here for almost thirty years.

Prohibition put an end to the brewery business, which had provided Will's livelihood. In 1919 he embarked upon a new enterprise, operating a fishing station and ice house in Santo Domingo (Dominican Republic). His family remembered this as a financial disaster, with Will returning home to New York in less than a year. Will then went to work as a salesman for Moeller's Malt Tonic, a non-alcoholic beer.

By this time, both of Will's sons had become successful businessmen, Wallace in sales and Clarence, after working for several years in Puerto Rico, as an executive with Bordo Products, a food processing company in Chicago.

With the end of prohibition in 1933, Will's job at Moeller's Malt Tonic came to an end. In the midst of the Depression Will was unable to find work in New York. Will and Louisa were forced to move in with Clarence in Chicago. Clarence eventually found his father a position as a plant supervisor at Bordo Products. However, when Clarence was forced out of Bordo in the late 1930s, Will also had to leave.

Will was seventy years old at the time. Lying about his age, he found employment with Bell and Howell on the production line, and worked there until retiring at the age of eighty-eight in 1955.

In 1948 a fire gutted Will and Louisa's Chicago apartment, on Howard Avenue. What was not burned was soaked in water. How this diary and the photos survived remains a mystery. Perhaps Will had already passed them on to his son, Clarence.

By the time Will retired from Bell and Howell in 1955, Clarence was divorced and living in Puerto Rico, where the cost of living was substantially less than Chicago. Will and Louisa joined him there in 1957 to enjoy a more comfortable retirement. Long before this, Louisa had been suffering from senile dementia, probably Alzheimer's disease.

In 1959 Will and Clarence settled in Los Angeles to be near Clarence's son Bill (Will's namesake). Louisa, too ill to travel, died in Puerto Rico shortly thereafter. Less than a year later, on August 2, 1960, Will died also. He collapsed of a heart attack while shaving one morning in the apartment he shared with Clarence.

❨

Will Shape's diary of his year in the Klondike gives us a picture of a fascinating individual. However, this alone is not a complete picture.

Once I realized the importance of Shape's Klondike diary, I felt an obligation to gather whatever additional information on him I could. Bill and Eunice Shape made available Shape's diary of his trip to Europe in 1885, family albums, and letters. In addition, before he passed away in the early

1990s, I conducted several oral interviews with Bill. I learned that Bill had often spent summers with his grandparents in their New York apartment when he was young. In addition, while growing up in Chicago, his grandparents were an integral part of an extended family there. Will's last year was spent in close proximity to Bill, who had moved to Los Angeles after World War II. Thus, Bill had many memories of his grandfather, spanning over forty years.

His grandchildren gave Will the nickname "Grandpa Foxy." This is likely an allusion to "Foxy Grandpa," the popular cartoon character of the 1920s. Foxy Grandpa was always outsmarting his adversaries (often his pesky grandkids) with his mental and physical dexterity.

Above all, Will was a person who enjoyed adventure and was always seeking a way to "make it." The Klondike trip was characteristic of an entrepreneurial drive throughout his life. "He was always trying to do something," in the words of Bill Shape. Thus, his Klondike trip was not an aberration.

Other events in his life demonstrate he was not afraid of the unknown, and adapted to varying circumstances. Fascinated by the world around him he was a keen observer of both the natural and man-made environments. Bill remembered his grandfather as even-tempered, but headstrong. "What he wanted to do, he did." Certainly, Will chose to follow his own path in life.

His tastes ranged from classical music to working with his hands. He was articulate and intelligent. However, he was not arrogant. Although he continued to search for the end of the rainbow that eluded him in the Klondike, he spent most of his life working for others.

Physically, he was not especially large or strong. Standing 5'8", he was never heavy. However, clearly demonstrated by his Klondike trip, he was hardy. Somewhat sickly as a youth, Will felt that his Northern trek actually improved his health. He attributed his longevity to a lifelong ritual of eating an apple while sitting in a bathtub of cold water prior to bed. Although he enjoyed good health, he occasionally suffered from attacks of "neuralgia." Never a "boozer," he did enjoy an occasional highball or beer. He was vigorous up until his death at age ninety-three. Even in old age, he never used a cane.

In Bill's memory, his grandfather was a sharp dresser. He always wore a long-sleeved shirt, with a coat and tie. Throughout his adult life, he wore wire-rim glasses. He was bearded during his Yukon trip, as were most, for convenience and protection from the elements. He also wore a mustache as a young man, but was clean shaven during the remainder of his life. Will loved to play cards, especially pinochle and bridge.

He enjoyed jokes, and was never "sour," even under adversity.

Although Will generally kept his politics to himself, he was active in the Republican Party. With his connections, he obtained a letter of introduction for his son Clarence from Wisconsin congressmen Gustav Küsterman. Clarence used this when he went to Puerto Rico as a young man. Will was also a lifelong member of the Masonic Lodge.

Will was respected as a hard worker, but Bill recollected that his grandmother lamented what might have been financially. Will had a reputation for accumulating cash, then heading off on a venture of some sort.

Will never lamented the choices he made. If his Klondike trip is typical, he seemed satisfied with his attempt, regardless of the outcome. He derived pleasure from his immediate circumstances, with any ultimate goal perhaps being secondary.

He carried the educational and cultural advantages of his youth throughout his life. Unlike his Klondike trip, Will's trip to Europe in 1885 included many cultural activities, especially concerts and the opera. In addition to competency on the cello, Will also played piano and ocarina. Bill had fond memories of his grandfather playing the piano and cello in the music room of their New York apartment. Will's recording of Yukon bird songs in musical notation in his diary indicates his familiarity with music.

Will enjoyed working with his hands. Perhaps typical of his creativity and energy was one of his hobbies as he approached the age of ninety: he made canes out of graduated shark vertebrae. Each required considerable work, and he sent finished canes to various celebrities, including Art Linkletter, Arthur Godfrey, and President Dwight Eisenhower. Will also enjoyed gardening, tending two Victory gardens as long as ten years after World War II.

Will Shape was also an artist. In his later years, he painted one watercolor every day. None of his work survives; 300 were destroyed when his Chicago apartment burned in 1948.

Perhaps as revealing as what Will did record in his diaries is what he chose to exclude. In both journals, there is little revealed of a personal nature; no introspection or "inner thoughts." He recorded his father's death in Switzerland as a matter of fact. From this approach to the world, it would appear that Will Shape was practical and rational, with little heed paid to emotions.

Judged by today's cultural values, Will might be considered racist. Certainly, his attitudes towards the native people he encountered in the North were condescending and ethnocentric. He does admit that those he dealt with were largely degraded as a result of their contact with whites. Still, by today's standards, it is embarrassing to read some of his passages regarding these encounters. However, it is important to witness and understand the attitudes of one hundred years ago.

We are still left with an incomplete picture of Will Shape. One wonders what perspective the observations of his companion, George, might provide. Was it the hardships of the trip that drove George to his seemingly irrational behavior? What idiosyncrasies of Will would we find unbearable under such circumstances?

In the end, Will Shape's Klondike journey was a small part of a rich and long life. For an unfortunate few, this trip was the end of their lives. For others, it was a high point. "Sourdough" reunions were popular for many years, catering to a group that continued to revel in its adventure. Will seems to have simply gotten on with his life, content that he had made the trip to the North.

No doubt, Will Shape would be proud to know that, through the publication of his diary and photos, he would reach a much wider audience than he originally intended. However, as a person willing to "think big," it is not likely he would be shocked to see this in print. Regardless, he was not the kind of person who would allow this to go to his head.

Anyone who reads his Klondike diary will probably feel a kinship with Will Shape. It is an intimate account of an important year. With his casual acceptance of hardship, his diary may not reflect the dangers and difficulties encountered by those who made this journey. However, it is an excellent account of an experience that we now celebrate, one hundred years later, as a test of the human capacity to withstand adversity in pursuit of material gain. Hopefully, as Will Shape did, you will come away enriched for sharing in his adventure.

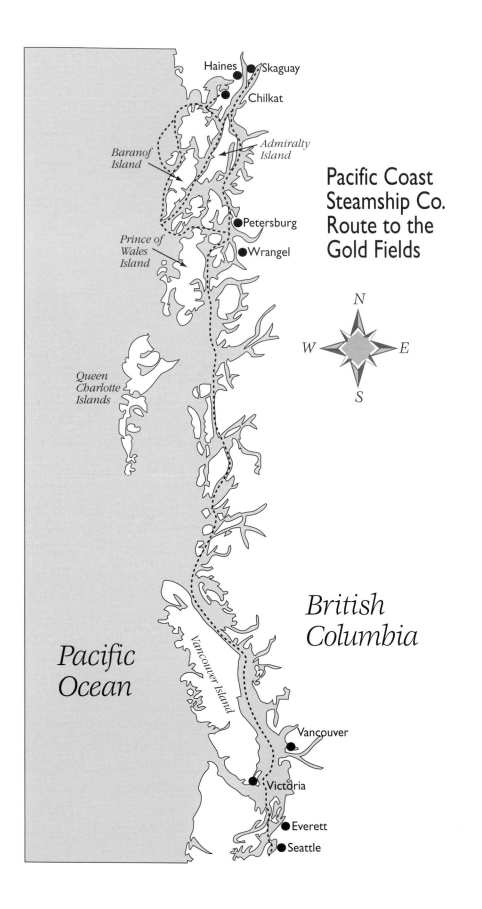

Pacific Coast
Steamship Co.
Route to the
Gold Fields

Seattle and the Inland Passage

Aug. 1897.

MY OBJECT IN writing up a description of this trip is for the purpose of giving my friends an idea of the endurance and hardship one experiences on a jaunt of this kind—not to say anything of the numerous disappointments, risks, etc. During the summer of 1897 the gold fever was at its height. I had heard and read so much about the gold fields, that I began to think seriously of joining the horde of gold hunters flocking to the far north and two weeks later had fully made up my mind.

My companions were George Hartmann of Brooklyn and the Oppenheimer brothers of New York City.

After purchasing our heavy clothing, footwear, tools, medicine chest, etc., we finally left New York on Tuesday, August 24th. The route as mapped out was from New York to Seattle by rail then via steamer to Haines Mission (a little Indian village located on Lynn Canal, Alaska) and from there on over the "Dalton Trail," to Five Finger Rapids with a pack train of oxen. After that we could take the complete outfit to Dawson City on rafts, sell our cattle and locate somewhere along Stewart River where prospects seemed pretty good. Sad indeed was the final parting from the Dear Ones we left behind, perhaps—never to see again.

We traveled over the D.L. & W.* & Nickel Plate R.R. to Chicago—next via Wis. Central to St. Paul and from there on to Seattle in a tourist car over the Great Northern R.R., and taking in the Dakota ranches; Missouri River; the splendid scenery along the Rocky Mountains; Kootenai River with its innumerable rapids and falls and the great "Switch Back" in Washington. (The Switch Back derives its name from a succession of short zigzag runs up the mountain side on steep grades. The train climbs one grade then backs up the next and so on until the top of the mountain is reached.)

Our meals en route were supplied from the lunch baskets we carried with us and the tea and coffee prepared on the range in the car. At some of the stations, little boys offered us wild ducks at 25 cts. a pair and no time was lost getting in a supply of them which the porter roasted for us in fine style.

Sunday the 28th we arrived in Seattle and stopped at the Commercial Hotel. Our Steamer (*Queen*—Capt. Carroll) did not leave until Sept. 8th, which gave ample time to select our stock of provisions and the cattle, sleds, pans, picks and shovels, etc.

Our provisions consisted of flour, beans, rice, oatmeal, cornmeal, sugar, bacon, hard tack, canned meats and evaporated fruits

*Delaware, Lackawanna & Western

and vegetables (1600 lbs.). Besides this, we carried a complete camping outfit, 6 ft. whip saw and large cross cut saw, packsaddles, tarpaulins, a .44 Winchester rifle, shot gun, revolvers and a number of books. One day when calling on the Captain, he informed us that there were no facilities for landing our outfit at the Mission outside of the ships boats—the cattle must swim ashore. When the O. brothers heard this they at once lost all interest in the trip, so George and I made up our minds to go on alone.

Opportunity was afforded us to visit Tacoma, Olympia and West Seattle. (The latter town is just opposite Seattle, 3 $\frac{1}{2}$ miles away.) Part of the time was passed in fishing for salmon out in the sound with a row-boat and trolling line (spook hook). Some of the fish we caught weighed from 8 to 12 lbs. And this is no fish story either (a little further on in the story, you will perhaps begin to think that I am exaggerating on the fish question, but everything is related just as it occurred). A 7 or 8 lb. salmon costs only 10 cts. in the fish market here.

Having heard so much about the cheap Japanese restaurants in Seattle, we could not resist the temptation to sample one of them. The following is a list of what was served for 15 cts.; clam chowder; salmon, served with an onion and a slice of lemon; boiled potatoes or chips; bread; corncake; one bun; radishes; tea and butter. (George and I figured for 6 months after that what the profit per meal was, but it was a vain attempt. While not served in Delmonica style, yet the food was well cooked and wholesome.)

Early in the morning on Sept. 8th our cattle was taken aboard the steamer—but not before the leader (a fine Jersey bull) had performed some interesting stunts on the dock; he was a little wild. The balance of our cattle consisted of 2 steers and 2 fine oxen, costing altogether $246.00 and the freight was $20.00 per head. Our fare was $25.00 each (first class) including #150 baggage. At 12 o'clock noon, amid the cheering of the vast crowd assembled on the dock, the *Queen* backed out into the sound and soon we were well on our way to the North. We were now thinking seriously of the long trip and hard work yet to come.

It was rainy, disagreeable weather to begin with, but later in the afternoon we had a glimpse of the cheery sunshine.

Port Townsend (a Port of Entry) was the first landing place; we stopped there 3 hours. Victoria (B.C.) was reached by night (another delay of 3 hours). Next came Union (B.C.) where the steamer took on coal. Nothing of interest is to be seen along this part of the route excepting the fine stretches of rich timber land along Georgia Bay. Our meals consisted of beef, veal, stew, soup, beans, oatmeal, potatoes, coffee and tea, bread, biscuits and butter. Breakfast was served at 7—lunch at 11:15 and supper at 4:30. On the morning of the 11th, just before reaching Mary's Island (U.S. Custom House) a heavy fog was encountered and the steamer was out of its course for several hours. The route leads along the narrow channels, between islands and rocks and is a dangerous one in heavy weather. To the right lies the main land and on the left an endless chain of islands, with here and there an open view of the ocean. We see mountains all along here, the slopes of which are covered with vast pine forests. When the fog finally cleared away the Captain was quite close to the rocky shore of Mary's Island. A sharp turn to the right brought the *Queen* around the point of the island, where the Customs officials, who had heard the signals, were awaiting us. After a hasty inspection of the captain's papers we continued on our course. The next stop was Gravina Point, where I saw the first salmon cannery. Only a short stop was made here and finally at 11 p.m. we arrived at Fort Wrangell, where the steamer was docked for the night. This gave us a chance to get ashore and we were very glad of the opportunity. Fort Wrangell is situated on an island and the town proper stretches along the base of a mountain. Here we find an Indian Mission; also several churches and stores (all of frame), a saw mill and last but not least, a brewery. It need hardly be mentioned that a large party paid the latter a visit. Beer is served in qt. measure at 2 bits (25 cts.). The Totem Poles of the Indians were found interesting. They represent weird images, which are carved in a solid tree—sometimes 4 or 5 one over the other. This is a good fur market—Mr. Maurice is the principal dealer. There are also a great many saloon gambling-houses and theatres. The genuine Alaskan dogs are numerous. Groups of Indians (homely and extra homely) sit around the doorsteps of their homes and display their stock of moccasins, snow-shoes, fur caps, horn ladles etc., which is offered for

sale. One thing that surprised me was the fact that some of the gardens contained patches of vegetables and the windows of many of the houses are adorned with flowers. Fish, such as salmon and halibut is very plentiful. The old military fort, from which the town derives its name, is still in fairly good condition.*

At 12 o'clock noon next day the steamer left Ft. W. and at 2 p.m. we passed through the Rainier Straits, or Narrows, a dangerous bit of water, particularly when the tide is running. The steamer winds its course around the islands, between hidden rocks and a number of buoys, which mark the direct route. We saw several whales this p.m.—also porpoise. Ducks, by the thousand, also snipe are found all along here.

Great chunks of ice (precipitated into the water from some glacier)** lined the shore and the mountains are covered with snow. The poor coffee and fatty food upset my stomach completely—our only good food was the stew, bread and tea. Our oxen gave us no end of trouble and worry.

Their stalls were ranged along the hatch on the middle deck and during the night they would batter down the board on front of [the] stall and next morning we found them standing outside, right close to the open hatch. It was very warm down there for them and they suffered considerable. Feeding and watering them was quite a task. The hay was mixed up with everybody else's down in the hold and water had to be

---

*The United States established Fort Wrangell in 1868. Previously, Russia had established Fort Dionysius here.
**LeConte Glacier

carried from the kitchen along the deck to where the stalls were—but before we could reach our pets we were compelled to climb along 3 or 4 rows of stalls to the rear of our own. About 2 buckets a piece was considered a moderate portion.

Later on we obtained our water from the upper deck and lowered it down the hatch to the middle deck, by means of a rope. George was a little careless one day in detaching the rope from the bucket and accidentally dropped the bucket into the hold, where one of the crew was at work assorting freight. Luckily for George the bucket barely missed the sailor—but in its downward flight it had turned over and the water was spilled all over him. (I will omit the sailor's remarks here.) I laughed until my sides ached, for George was in great despair and his profuse apologies were drowned by the sailor's rapid fire of curses.

We have had rain almost continually and but for these little incidents, one of which I just related, the trip would have been rather monotonous. The steamer arrived at Juneau at 11 p.m. and again tied up to the town dock for the night. Here again we were permitted to go ashore to see the town. Juneau, like Ft. Wrangell is located at the base of a mountain. It is a typical mining town—has some large stores and theatres, gambling houses and low resorts of all kinds; but more saloons than anything else. Beer costs 15 cts. or 2 for 25 cts., whiskey 25 cts., cigars from 10 cts. up.

Some of our fellow passengers left the vessel here intending to take the Stikeen Route, which leads from the mouth of

Stikeen River, opposite Juneau.*

At 10 a.m. on the 13th we left Juneau and landed at Douglas Island, just across the bay.

The famous Treadwell Gold Mining Co. (quartz mine) is located here. Its buildings cover a large tract of land. It is a 300 stamp mill and we were informed that there is enough quartz here to keep the mill busy for 50 years to come. The town is located some little distance from the dock. Indian huts are scattered all along the water front and their occupants are a filthy lot. The steamer *Alki* of the same line, left the island at 12 o'clock and as our captain was anxious to reach Skaguay ahead of her, only part of the freight for this point was unloaded and at 1:30 we were off again for Skaguay. (At that time there were no docks at Skaguay—all freight was dumped on a big scow and then hauled ashore at high tide.) Haines Mission is only 15 miles this side of Skaguay, and since we were the sole passengers for that point, the Captain decided to take us along to the end of his route, get rid of his bulky freight and then unload our outfit on his return trip. The *Queen* is a fast boat and overhauled the *Alki* at 7 p.m. It was a fast run and everybody cheered as the slower boat was left a-stern.

We reached Skaguay at about 9 p.m. It was a fine bright night, but quite chilly. The high snow-covered mountains loomed up in the distance and it was here we got our first real glimpse of the grand scenery in Alaska. Wishing to see the town, we decided to spend a few hours on shore.

---

*The Stikeen (Stikine) route actually left from Wrangell. The Taku route left from Juneau.

Climbing into a boat, we were rowed up quite a distance to the flats and then it was a case of wading through mud for a half mile before striking the town. The beach is low here with just a gentle upward slope toward Skaguay. The tide was also low and when the water fully receded, it left bare a number of mud flats and the distance from the water to town was fully $1^1/_2$ miles. There was not much of interest to be seen here;—a few stores, plenty of saloons, dance halls and gambling dens everywhere. Most of the inhabitants were living in tents, but there were also a number of frame-houses. We returned to the steamer at 1:30 in the morning, pretty well tired out and covered with mud.

By mistake our outfit was shifted to a large scow during the night, but the Captain had it transferred back to the steamer. Our supply of hay was just about exhausted when a good hearted fellow passenger offered to help us out with several bales of his own at Seattle prices. Hay cost 75 to $100 per ton here. Skaguay was not nearly so bad as the papers pictured it—all was quiet and orderly excepting the gambling dens and dives. We paid 50 cts. for the trip to town and back. All cattle and freight was loaded on an immense scow and assorted by the owners as it came aboard.

We bought 3 cans of marmalade from one of the kitchen hands for $1.00 and the fellow felt so good over it that he invited us to a fine cup of coffee and some pie in the fo'castle. During the trip we had often assisted the gardener in preparing his vegetables for the kitchen and in return for this favor he gave us a sack filled with potatoes, carrots and onions which came in very handy later on. One could buy most anything from the kitchen or pantry hands also.

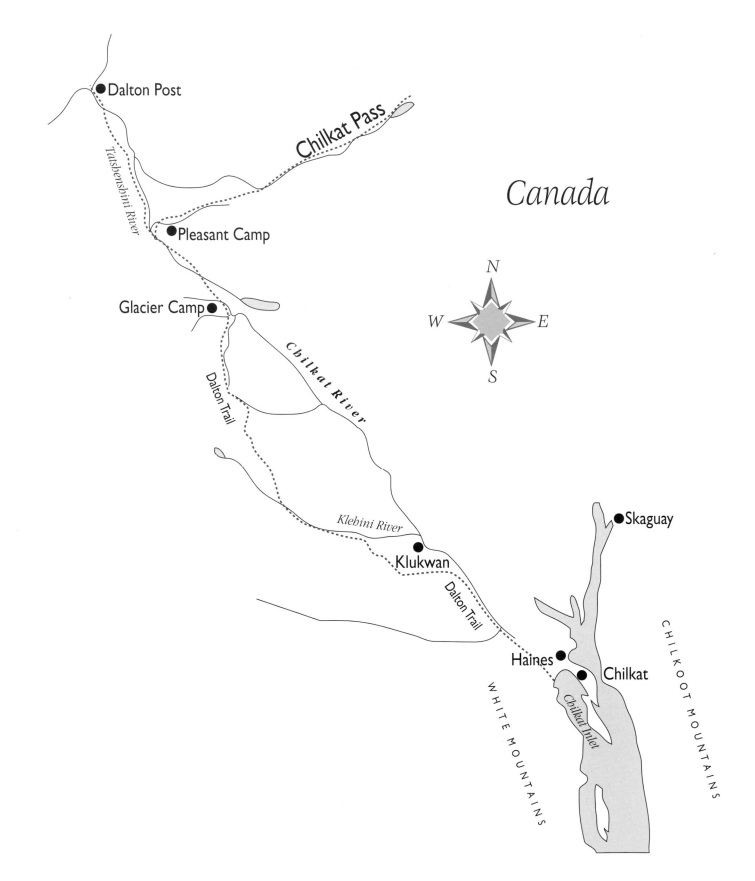

Canada

Dalton Post

Chilkat Pass

Tatshenshini River

Pleasant Camp

Glacier Camp

Dalton Trail

Chilkat River

N
W E
S

Klehini River

Skaguay

Klukwan

Dalton Trail

CHILKOOT MOUNTAINS

Haines

Chilkat

WHITE MOUNTAINS

Chilkat Inlet

Haines Mission and the Chilkat Pass

Chapter Two

Sept. 14.

FOR A CHANGE we have bright sunshine, but it is rather cool.

By 8:30 in the evening, all freight was unloaded and the steamer started back on the return trip, intending to let us off at Haines Mission. We arrived there at 9:30 and dropped anchor in the harbor. Here our real task was to begin. It was a dark night—there were no lights excepting the electric search-light on the steamer which the Captain had kindly ordered into service to assist us in finding our way to shore. We were now to be landed on this strange shore with nothing but Indians for companions. The only white people, as we discovered later on, were Mr. Warren* (the missionary), Mrs. Warren and 2 children, one servant, the matron at the school and Mr. Rogers (the carpenter).

There was no delay in the preparations for landing. A boat was lowered, manned by an officer, 4 of the crew and myself; George remained on board to see that nothing was left behind. The first steer was lowered in the horse-box which had a rope fastened to the trap door on the front. Another rope was fastened to the steer's horns and I held the end of that in the boat. When the box reached the water, the trap door was pulled open by one of the crew on deck and Mr.

*Rev. W.W. Warren

Steer plunged into the water, splashing about and snorting. I hauled him up close to the boat, holding his head above water and the crew pulled for shore, 300 yds. away. This steer could swim like a fish and made several desperate attempts to get away—it was all I could do to hold him up close. Once or twice he did get his horns under the boat and threatened to make things lively for us. He was landed safely at the beach, however, and hurriedly tied to the first log I could reach. Then we returned for number 2—he was landed without any trouble. The third one was a poor swimmer and could barely stand the strain of a long swim in ice cold water. We had given up all hope of landing him alive, as he rolled over on his sides a few times and was completely winded from over-exertion. His head was held up however and I heaved a deep sigh of relief when he too was landed safely. He was unsteady on his legs, so I left him standing there to think it over. The remaining two were good swimmers and we had no further trouble. Next our provisions were landed and George also came ashore. After tipping off the crew and shaking hands all around, with many good wishes for success, we were left alone, to shift for ourselves, in total darkness. The crew hastily returned to the steamer, which tooted her last farewell and was soon lost from view. In our hurry to land the outfit, we neglected to tie up two of the beasts and they had wandered off down the beach and into the woods with a pack of Indian dogs in pursuit. We started out after them & in a half hours time had the unruly critters securely tied with the rest. The next thing to be attended to was our provisions; for the tide was fast coming in and had almost reached our goods. To make matters worse it began to rain pretty hard. Hardly had we removed one row of goods, when the water was already close to the next lot. Some of the heavy packages we could not handle, so one of the oxen was made to pull them up by means of a pack-saddle and some rope. We worked like beavers, placed all of the goods on high ground and then hastily pitched our tent. It was 2 a.m. when we retired for the night, drenched to the skin and completely tired out. For a bed we used a few sacks of flour and spread blankets over them. Not even our clothes were changed—we were too tired for that and slept until 9 o'clock.

I must mention right here that I never enjoyed a better night's sleep in my life. There were quite a number of Indians living in tents along the beach where our outfit was landed. We paid no attention to them however, and they did not annoy us either.

The first morning some of the old bucks and squaws with their little ones came around to look us over and to our surprise we found that a few of them could speak broken English—so it did not take us long to form their acquaintance. They would however always make use of the native tongue when conversing among themselves, which was annoying to us—but we got even by talking German, so they could not understand us either. The Mission consisted of a school and church at one end of the village; also the minister's house and stables. Further down the beach were some log and frame houses where many of the Indians lived.

The Rev. Mr. Warren was a kind-hearted, pleasant gentleman, not over 40 years of age, who offered to assist us in any way possible. Mr. Rogers was also very good to us and we spent considerable time in his company. A few days were spent in repacking our goods and experimenting as to the best method of getting them over the trail.

It rained every day, which made things a bit gloomy.

Sept. 19.

Just for an experiment we commenced to load our outfit on the pack-animals and discovered that we had too much weight for them to carry. Thus we were compelled to dispose of a large quantity of provisions and whatever else could be spared. Then our oxen were not trained and it required lots of muscles and patience to break them in. Our method was to tie the unruly ones by the horns up close to a tree—then fasten the pack-saddle and load up 200 lbs. and let them think it over. At first they would buck, kick and snort, making things lively generally, but it soon dawned on them that they could neither get away nor throw off the pack.

On the 19th most of the Indians went away in their canoes—some to Juneau, 100 miles down the canal and others to Dyea, 15 miles above Haines Mission. Many of the Indians attended church yesterday (being Sunday), and we were quite busy disposing of provisions at cost price.

Our tent was packed with old bucks and their squaws all day long. Every Indian asked for sugar first—next tobacco. They are an ignorant lot, excepting when it comes to a trade; they want to buy cheap, but always ask a good price for their own goods. (In Indian tongue a-cu means "come here", chuck-tu, "go-away" and muck-muck, "food".) When some certain article strikes their fancy, they ask the price. It may suit them, but they never show it, offer something less and walk away. After awhile Mr. Indian comes back, looks over the article again, but makes no better offer. If you have the patience to wait long enough, you can perhaps make the sale.

Mr. Rogers had warned us not to undertake our long journey inland at this season of the year, but the Thorpe* outfit consisting of 200 head of cattle and 60 horses, bound for Dawson City had preceded us by 8 days and we surely could catch up with them, as we believed. The Chilkat Pass (not Chilkoot), which must be crossed before the snow storms come on was just about 40 miles from here. Several trips were made to the village of Chilkat (which lies just 1 ½ miles over the hill from the Mission, at the mouth of Chilkat River).

There are 2 stores there—one owned by Col. Sol Ripinsky and the other by Koehler

---

*Willis Thorpe, a Juneau butcher, grew wealthy by supplying beef to Dawson.

and James. Jack Dalton, of Dalton Trail fame, also lives here in a comfortable frame house. The balance of the inhabitants are Indians. Pyramid Harbor is just opposite Chilkat, on the river.

Sept. 20.

This day we commenced our overland trip. It was raining and stormy weather—the trail was in a frightful condition. Our oxen got stuck in the mud in several places up to their bellies and this with packs on their backs. There are no streets here—nothing but footpaths or cattle trails to follow. Our fun was just beginning. Whenever the oxen were stuck, it was only by incessant urging and vigorous application of a stout stick, that we succeeded in forcing them to extricate themselves from the rut. They finally did this with great effort and slowly wriggle out of the mire on their knees. No one realizes how hard we worked to save our provisions from getting soaked in the water and mud. The trail was a very narrow one, leading through the woods—because the pack-animals could not get through the woods with the bulky packs on their backs.

Our leader, the Jersey bull, broke away at one point and ran helter skelter through the woods, disarranging the entire pack. Geo. chased after him and after some lively sprinting managed to corner the beast, and led him back into line. Geo. was mad clean through, but I could not help laughing—it was such a funny sight. We now tied the animals by the horns, five in a row. The bull had a ring snapped in his nose so we could manage him better. One man led the way leading the bull on a rope and the other one followed the outfit, keeping them moving by vigorous application of the stick, twisting of tails, etc. The trail, as I have already explained, was a narrow one and full of mud holes.

We found it very difficult to keep the animals in line, especially as one of the steers took a notion to ram his head up against any tree which happened to stand near the trail and there he would stick—head down and snorting, holding the whole train in check.

Club him as we might, this terror would not remove his head from the tree, until he got good and ready. The English vocabulary does not contain all the words we used on such an occasion. The high rubber boots we wore felt as heavy as lumps of lead after a long tramp.

The outfit contained a sheet iron stove and 2 sleds, which made very unhandy packages, projecting out from the side of the pack and every now and then the train was halted and the packs rearranged. It was very near night before we found a good camping ground that day.

Our stove pipes had in some way become detached from one of the packs and were lost on the way. The cattle was turned loose to graze; the tent pitched in a hurry and then after partaking of a big supper we immediately retired to our sleeping bags to enjoy a good night's rest.

Next day I returned to Chilkat for a new stove pipe, a 2 1/2 hrs. tramp. I followed up the Chilkat River half the distance and then intending to shorten my route, started straight over the mountain, where I lost my way among the mass of thick brush, fallen trees and shrubbery. While skirmishing around, I discovered a fine patch of blueberries and rested for half an hour munching berries; they were delicious.

With the sun for my guidance I hastened on and finally arrived at Chilkat in the afternoon. Not wishing to waste any time, I bought the stove pipe and a few other things, intending to return to camp in a canoe but not one Indian would accommodate me, although I offered up to $3.00 for this service. So I decided to walk back via Haines Mission. Great was my surprise, when on the way over I met a little Indian lad who was carrying our lost stove pipe—evidently bound for one of the stores, where he wanted to sell it. I at once claimed the pipe and gave him 50 cts. for his trouble. (Stove pipe cost 50 cts. a length here.)

My load was now too heavy for me to carry alone, so I hired an Indian for $1.50 to assist me in packing my goods back to camp.

Our camp was located near Clark's place, on Chilkat River. (Clark was a white man, who was living with a squaw.) He lived in a nice frame house, had a barn on his premises and made a living by selling vegetables to the Indians, who are too lazy and have no patience for such things.

Clark had two children—a boy and a girl of 10 and 6 yrs. respectively and Mrs. Clark was a good looking pleasant woman of perhaps 35 yrs. and spoke English fairly well. She invited us to a meal of corned beef and cabbage which we enjoyed very much. We did not cover much ground thus far, on account of the trouble and delay with the cattle—so it was thought best to let an Indian take our goods up the river in a canoe, so we could drive the cattle over the trail without packs, thus gaining considerable time. The Indian was hired for $34.00 ($2.00 per 100 lbs. to Klukwan, an Indian village some distance up the river) and $10.00 extra for permission to use his canoe in crossing two channels, which were too wide and deep to be forded.

Sept. 22.

On the move again. George went up in the canoe, to watch over the goods, together with the old Indian, squaw, little girl and boy, while I hired another Indian for a guide and drove the cattle over the trail. All they carried was the pack-saddles. After travelling along 3 or 4 miles, we came to a cluster of rocks near the water's edge, where all further progress was blocked.

The Indian had either lost his way, which was not at all likely or he had led me astray on purpose. I realized this and would have given the fellow a good drubbing if it were not for the possible trouble we might have with the Indians.

Retracing our steps to a point $^{1}/_{4}$ mile below, I found that he should have taken the mountain trails there, instead of following along the river bank. It was then 2 o'cl. P.M. and the canoe at least 2 miles ahead of us, clean out of sight.

There was no way I could communicate with Geo. except by firing my revolver.

I tried that 3 or 4 times and the shots were heard and answered. (We had previously agreed on a signal.) Knowing that some one of the party would return to us, I had it out with the Indian in the meantime, for leading me astray. He acted as though he did not understand me and offered all sorts of excuses, which had no bearing whatever on the case and I could do nothing with him.

After waiting patiently for an hour, the Indian boy hove in sight and gave me to understand that the rest were returning and would camp with us.

Geo. arrived an hour later and soon after that the Indian located us also. It was now too late for a fresh start, so we turned the cattle loose and camped for the night. The guide was promptly discharged and received but $1.50 for his poor services. (He had asked $3.00 a day.) We thought it a wiser plan to look after the cattle ourselves and allow the Indian to take care of our goods in the canoe.

One part of the trail was full of sharp rocks, which cut the hoofs of the cattle.

At some places fallen trees overhung the trail and the oxen had difficulty in jamming by this obstruction. Two of the pack-saddles were smashed in this fashion, by catching on trees.

We had a very muddy trail, dotted in many places with these sharp pointed rocks.

One of the oxen turned a complete somersault, slipping on a steep grade and landing on his side with a crash. (He broke one of his ribs in this fall, as we discovered later on.) At another place where the narrow trail cut across a steep grade, our leader lost his footing and slipped down off the path, threatening to pull the other four after him. The rope he had fastened to his horns was hastily cut and our fine bull rolled down the grade until he encountered a tree in his path, which put a very sudden check to his trip. He was then quite safe for the time being—but for the tree he might have rolled on down to the bottom of the mountain.

First of all the other four were driven to a place of safety and then we returned for the bull. It required fully $^1/_2$ hours hard work to get him up the grade, but the train was soon on the move again. Night was coming on and our animals were pretty well used up—still we had quite some distance to travel before striking the down grade which brought us to the valley below, where the Indian was, no doubt, already awaiting us. The oxen were pulled and clubbed along, all the way; up, as well as down the grade. When the steep down grade was finally reached, night was upon us. Our oxen were very stubborn and afraid to go down the narrow path, never knowing when they might slip off.

We took an awful chance, but intense hunger and thirst urged us onward. Only by incessant urging and clubbing could we manage to keep them moving. (Quite heroic treatment, to be sure, but it was the only one under the circumstances.)

No one can realize what hard work it was. Finally we did reach the valley below and after wading across a meadow (which was flooded with water, one ft. deep) and several streams, we met our friend, the Indian, who had come to greet us and show

the way to the beach. He had a good fire started for us, and after turning the cattle loose, we hastily prepared a supper, consisting of bacon, hard-tack, coffee and a little fruit. (I'll never forget how good this meal tasted.) Being too tired to put up our own tent, we simply spread our sleeping-bags under the Indian's shelter, taking particular care not to get too close to his blankets, for fear of the vermin he had in them.

During the night two of our oxen had wandered away and nearly an hour was wasted next morning in locating them. They were found some distance away, in the woods, quietly feeding, yet unwilling to return—but we brought them back in a hurry.

Sept. 24.

Our first task this day was to cross several wide and deep channels. In vain did we try to drive the cattle across—they would wade out into the stream until the deep channel was reached and then turn back suddenly, making for the shore. To make short work of their antics we finally tied a rope to their horns, so all were compelled to follow the leader, who had a long rope fastened to his horns. The Indian carried the end of this rope across [the] stream in his canoe.

When all was ready we drove the cattle into the stream and the Indian pulled at the rope from the opposite bank. This scheme worked like a charm. But while driving them out into deep water, I ventured out a little too far, accidentally stepping into a deep hole and lost my footing.

The current carried me down stream and I was forced to swim. It was a close call, but with a mighty effort I managed to reach the shore some short distance below. Drenched to the skin and shivering with cold, I sat down beside the camp-fire with the squaw and her baby, trying to warm up a bit. There was no time for a change of clothes however, as we had another wide channel to cross, besides unnumerable smaller ones, the canoe being brought into service three times.

We were now on the mud flats along Chilkat River, which extend between the various channels. (The river bed here is about a mile wide—there is one deep channel and a great many smaller ones running in all directions.)

It was here the treacherous quicksand was encountered and several times our cattle got right into the worst of it. Quick work was required to keep them moving along, for a minute's delay might mean the loss of an ox or two. Standing on one spot for a few moments only, one could see the ground slowly receding and the water oozing out all around. In less than ten minute's time you would be covered up and disappear entirely under the surface. What work was required to keep the cattle from sinking here can better be imagined than described.

It was 6:30 before we at last camped in some woodland near the river bank and I had the opportunity to change my wet clothes. Aside from a severe cold of short duration I felt no ill effects from the ducking I received this morning.

It rained some in the evening, but having previously gathered in a lot of dry wood, we were enabled to keep up a good fire all night. Our Indian friends had salmon, as usual, for supper and we helped them out with some coffee which they enjoyed immensely. When the Indian wants a fish he takes his long slender pole, with a bent hook fastened to the end of it and wades out into the stream, waiting for the salmon to come along. (He could see a fish where I could not see it in a year.) When the fish is located, his pole swings through the air like a flash and the sharp hook digs into its side. There is no escape for that fish and very seldom the Indian misses his prey.

Sometimes we found a stream in which the current was unusually swift and deep water. In such cases we just climbed on the back of one of the oxen and let him carry us over. If we missed this method, then our only salvation was to catch hold of his tail and let him pull us over. (It required considerable force to hang on to the tail, too.)

The oxen gradually grew accustomed to the water and would cross a stream without hesitation.

Sept. 25.

A-qual-tu, the next Indian settlement was our destination this day, so we arose at 5:30 in order to get an early start.

Before proceeding with the story of this trip, however, I want to say something about our friends, the Indians. There are some things that occurred here and there—some very funny and others very serious, but this one is really too good to be forgotten and it may be of interest.

When our friends retire for the night they do not put up a tent the same as we, but just a wall of canvas fixed up with two poles, to keep off the wind. Then they pile in under their blankets, all in a heap. The first thing they do every morning after breakfast (lucky for us it happened after breakfast and not before) is to gather up their blankets and pick off the lice, all hands assisting in the job. It was really interesting to watch them, they were such experts at this business. They did not kill them however, simply threw them away. (We were told that the Indians considered it a sin to kill them, but don't know if this is true or not.)

This day we waded a great many streams and puddled through the mud flats all day long. It was very tiresome work and our cattle too were pretty well played out. It was 3 P.M. when we reached a barren flat, just opposite A-qual-tu, on the river bank and here our tent was pitched.

In the last stretch of 10 miles, we waded some 40 odd channels. The total distance covered thus far was 20 miles of the worst trail imaginable. Five days and a quarter was the actual traveling time, but this of course included many delays, while en route. The weather was quite pleasant during the day, but the nights were always very cool. Our oxen, all tired out and footsore, were led to the woods near by, where there was a scanty supply of grass and leaves.

Sept. 27.

The scenery all along here is fine—on either side of the river are high mountains, covered with spruce forests.

Our broken pack-saddles were repaired and everything put in trim for the further trip. The Indian and his family left us here and started out for the homeward trip. This morning we wished to drive the cattle to a better feeding ground and in doing so one of the oxen got stuck in a mud hole and could not extricate himself—he simply stuck fast, as though glued to the spot.

We hastily procured our shovels and dug away the mud from under him, also freed his legs as much as possible (for he was steadily sinking deeper) and after 4 1/2 hours of hard work, succeeded in getting him out. He did not step very far however before he again stuck fast in the soft clay. We worked like beavers to save that poor beast, for we had become so attached to the animals and could not bear the thought of losing any of them; especially in this manner.

But this was only the beginning of our troubles. Trying to pry him up out of the mud with logs was one of the many methods employed to extricate him. It was growing dark by this time and we could not work much longer, so after pushing some logs under his body, to keep him from sinking further, and covering him up with a blanket, we returned to camp for something to eat and a much needed rest.

Sept. 28.

Finding the ox in the same position this morning (up to his belly in mud) we again went to work with our shovels. By placing branches in the mud a few feet from his body, thus forming a sort of wall, the mud was prevented from flowing back under him. After again clearing away the mud around and under him, also along his legs, we found the beast too weak to pull himself loose.

In desperation a rope was fastened around his horns and hitched to another ox. The latter seemed to realize what was wanted of him, for he started to pull and never let up until he had the other one landed on high and solid ground.

It took us just 5 hours to accomplish this feat. Some of the Indians from the village had gathered around us, watching the operation and assisting us to the best of their ability. But they were all afraid of the ox, for every time he only turned his head around they would scatter in all directions, much to our amusement. I could not understand why these Indians, who go out into the woods after bear and moose should be so afraid of a perfectly harmless animal. The poor beast could not stand on its legs, for the long confinement in that mud hole not only stiffened his joints, but left him also in a weak condition. We discovered also that one of his ribs was broken in the fall over the rocks a few days ago and that no doubt added to his sufferings. Still we had hopes of bringing him around all right and after covering him well with a blanket, also placing some feed within easy reach, we returned to camp, $1/4$ mile away, all tired out, disgusted and hungry. (My appetite was ravenous—I could eat all the time.)

On a later visit the ox was found to be in much weaker condition and rather than let him suffer longer, we thought it best to end his misery. Two bullets from our revolver finished him. The Indians, it seemed had been expecting this, for no sooner were the shots fired, when a number of them came along on the full run, brandishing their knives and yelling like a lot of cowboys. We motioned to them to assist us in the job and after bleeding the ox, all hands joined in the skinning operation. It was our first experience in this sort of business, but that ox was skinned in short order. All the Indians, I noticed, were experts in handling a knife.

Each of the Indians received a chunk of meat in return for his services and they seemed to be immensely pleased. We cut the carcass into 6 parts and covered up the meat for the night.

The loss of this ox was a serious blow to us, for we could not pack the outfit on the remaining four; but there was no use grumbling—we expected to meet with reverses and difficult problems to overcome.

Sept. 29.

It had snowed some during the night and the weather was cold. A severe storm was raging and we expected our tent to be ripped up any moment, as the stakes did not hold very well in the sandy soil. So the camp was moved $1/4$ mile further up the trail into a fine patch of woods, where we were securely sheltered from the wind. The meat was packed on a sled and our faithful ox (the one that pulled the other ox out of the mud hole) hauled it up to camp where it was left out in the snow and covered with the hide.

This unexpected delay, at this point, spoiled our plans. Chilkat Pass 20 miles distant, was already covered with snow, at an elevation of 4,000 feet. Should we remain here, the cattle would starve, as good feed was very scarce—the oxen now feeding on dry grass and leaves. (We were told that the best time to start out over this trail with cattle is in June or July, when the fresh grass is plentiful.)

Oct. 1.

The weather has moderated some and we have 3 inches of snow on the ground.

Our goods were again repacked in preparation for a trip with the sleds, but the food problem worried us. If we could get over the coast mountains and save our cattle, perhaps there was a chance for us to get to some settlement where we could spend the Winter. But if the cattle would starve on the way it would surely be the end of the trip then and there.

It was a shame to let our lot of fresh meat go to waste and since we could not carry it with us we tried to dispose of it to the Indians. They pleaded poverty and referred us to their chief, Co-to-wah, who lived at Klukwan, 2 miles up the river.

(We have had good meals of late—such as oxtail soup with rice, boiled tongue, liver and bacon, kidney stew, etc.) Two meals daily is the rule.

We have a plentiful supply of dry wood on hand and our tent is kept warm and comfortable. Sea-gulls, ravens, eagles and ducks are numerous and the streams are fairly alive

with "Dog Salmon."* At this season of the year the water is low and we can see hundreds of fish, as they come down stream wriggling along over the sand and gravel bottoms in an effort to reach deeper water. When we wanted fish, we just waded out into the middle of the channel and whacked them with a stick. This sounds a little fishy, but it is true.

Sometimes, just for sport, we chased them in all directions and often they would jump right out of the water and land on the beach, for there was not enough water for them to swim in. The fish weighed anywhere from 4 to 10 or 15 lbs. but were not very good eating. Many of the larger fish got stuck on the sand and gravel and there was a regular stench from the dead fish. What amused me was to see the Siawash (Indian) dogs go into the water after fish. They would bite them in the back, shake them a few times and leave them on the beach just to amuse themselves.

The day we hauled our meat to the camp, one of these dogs sneaked up to our tent and carried away a kidney and part of the liver, which had been left outside in a bucket—we did not catch him in the act, however. These dogs steal anything within reach, from a piece of soap, or candle, up to a fine steak. The heart and liver were hung up in a tree, out of the dog's reach, but the birds feasted on it there. We had made up our minds to kill that dog if he ever turned up here again.

The kidney and liver must have suited his taste and the temptation was too much

---
*Chum salmon.

for him, for early next morning he paid us a second visit. George snatched up the Winchester and taking careful aim, ended his existence forever.

What a chance we were taking! Had the Indians discovered a wounded dog, they would surely make things interesting for us. We realized this and hastily buried him in the woods, covering up the spot with shrubs and leaves. There was one dog less in that section, at any rate.

My hands were so badly chapped and swollen, I could barely bend my fingers, but a liberal application of carbolic salve (one of the articles included in our medicine chest) put them in fairly good condition. My left foot was also sore and swollen and for the past week I have had a sharp pain in the side. But these are only slight ills—taking it all in all I am feeling well and my appetite is good.

Oct. 2.

Disappointment again—it rained all night long, the snow has disappeared and today the weather is bright and warm. We have no more hope of ever taking our cattle to "Five Fingers" alive. Just for a little diversion from the regular routine of camp life, we paid the Indians at (A-qual-tu) Katkwaltu a visit, with a view to disposing of our meat. The charge for crossing the river and back again in one of their canoes, was $1.00, none of them seemed over anxious to purchase the meat at any price. I bought a buck-skin suit from an old Indian whose only clothing was a shirt and drawers—besides he was barefooted and very dirty. Answering to my question as to his

age, he replied that he was 90 moons old (pointing to the sky). I guess he meant 90 yrs. For he was a very old fellow. We visited several of the shacks where the squaws were busily engaged in fancy bead-work on moccasins, sewing up blankets, etc.

They live in log huts, which are provided with bunks to sleep in. The floor is boarded, excepting for a square space in the centre, which is reserved for the fire-place. The smoke passes out through an opening in the roof, directly over the fire-place. Their meals are cooked in large kettles, which hang suspended from the ceiling on a wire or iron hook. The Indians are always scratching themselves—it gives one the itch to look at them.

One old buck, who looked more like a devil in disguise than a human being, was sitting on the floor, with his knees tucked up under his chin, greedily devouring a dish of fresh, raw salmon eggs with evident delight—the juice oozing from the corners of his mouth. I looked at George and his disgusted look made me smile. George said something in German, which I cannot repeat here. Anything and everything I have eaten up in this country so far, tasted good to me, but I would not attempt to eat those salmon eggs for a $100.00 bill. The sight of it nearly upset my stomach. We had seen enough of the Indians for one day and were mighty glad to get back to our humble tent.

Oct. 3.

It rained all day, so our time was spent in repairing the pack-saddles and baking bread. Our first attempt at baking, however, was a flat failure. We used some flour which Mrs. O. and my wife had prepared for us, to be used in an emergency. I don't doubt that the flour was all right, but the bread was as flat as a pancake (it did not raise a little bit) and was hard as a rock. We tried to eat just a little of it, but the attempt was a failure, since our teeth were to be preserved for future use.

Oct. 4.

Being desirous of meeting chief Co-to-wah, to whom we expected to sell our meat, we tramped up the river to Klukwan, where we were at once surrounded by a crowd of bucks, squaws and children, who greeted us in a friendly, but informal manner. (Their greetings always left me under the impression that a white man was not a very welcome guest.) One of the Indians led us to the chief's house and the latter beckoned us to enter. We found his home to be a comfortable log cabin and he had 3 or 4 young squaws living with him.

Another Indian served as interpreter, for Co-to-wah could not talk English. We were surprised to find a man of about 45 years, quite tall and well built, with a hardened face that never once smiled, and he was dressed in ordinary flannel shirt, pants, and slouch hat. First of all, he showed us a contract he had with the Alaska Packers' Ass'n., for the season's catch of fish. He proudly pointed to his name in the contract, giving us to understand that he was the real chief. In the contract the Ass'n. agreed to take from him all

the fish at the rate of $8.00 per 100. After a few preliminary exchanges of greetings, etc., the meat question was explained to him and he expressed a desire to look it over. Taking 3 Indians with him we all crossed the river in his canoe and started back for camp. On the way over one of his companions shot an eagle and proved himself an excellent marksman. The price we asked for the meat was $20.00, hide and all. Co-to-wah and his friends talked the matter over and offered $11.00 which was accepted. He wanted to bring his boat down the river and come back for the meat later on.

We waited patiently for several hours, but he failed to return or send any word. We came to the conclusion that he was playing a foxy game. Evidently he realized that we could not carry the meat along with us and so would be compelled to leave it behind for them to feast on, but he never made a greater mistake in his life—we were fully on to his trick.

Oct. 5.

Still no sign of the chief—we wanted to give him the benefit of the doubt and waited until evening without hearing from him. Then we built a big fire near camp and threw on the meat, burning it to a crisp—only reserving a supply for our own use and that settled the case for the foxy chief. During the night I was aroused from my sleep by some disturbance in the tent and upon awakening I discovered George sitting up, with a candle in one hand and a hatchet in the other, trying to kill a little mouse which he claimed had been walking all over him in his sleep. It was amusing to see him trying in vain to land on the little creature and at last gave up the task and pulled his blankets over his head.

Oct. 6.

Nothing of importance occurred this day until late in the afternoon when I happened to glance up the trail and discovered a lot of cattle and horses coming in our direction. We surmised at once that it was the Thorpe outfit, which had preceded us. Evidently they did not succeed in crossing the mountains and were forced to return to the coast.

And so it was—the boys told us not to attempt the passage of the mountains. They got as far as the summit, but were compelled to return on account of the fierce snow-storms that were raging there and for the further reason that there was no feed for the cattle. Seven horses were lost in one day and their packs left along the trail, just where the poor animals dropped. But Thorpe's son and 3 companions braved the storms, taking 10 pack-horses with them and pushing on inland. Thorpe's brother, we were told, was waiting for a supply of provisions at his claim, far in the interior. It was reported later on that these brave fellows managed to reach "Five Fingers," but with only 4 or 5 horses out of the ten. The Mahoney party, coming out overland from Dawson City and bound for Juneau, had also passed along here today and reported 125 miles of snow in one stretch, beyond the mountains.

The big outfit camped near us for the night and as the boys were all tired out and very hungry, we gave them a plentiful supply of fresh meat, which they consumed in short order.

All hope of reaching Stewart River this year was now abandoned. There was but one thing to do—return to the Mission and remain there until the season was favorable for going inland over the White and Chilkoot passes, which lead from Skaguay and Dyea, respectively.

Oct. 7.

The Thorpe outfit left here early this morning—some of the boys going down the river in canoes, while others took charge of the cattle.

Our goods were carried back to the river, where we intended to engage an Indian to take them down stream, as far as Clark's place, from which point we could have the cattle pack them back to the Mission. There were no canoes available however, and we were compelled to pitch our tent again and wait for 2 days in a drenching rain before one of the lazy Indians offered his services.

Oct. 9.

Our goods were packed into the canoe and left in charge of the Indian, while George and I drove the cattle back over the same route. Everything worked smoothly, until we struck quicksand in one of the streams. (We had crossed at this same spot before and found it safe.) The oxen got over it safely, but our bull got stuck and we could not budge him an inch. He was very stubborn also and did not make much of an effort to extricate himself. It was not safe to linger long on this treacherous ground and our oxen were becoming restless, for at every step they would sink down a foot or so. We tried to coax the bull, then applied the switch—all in vain. As a last resort the rope was tied, as in our previous experience, but he could not be budged an inch and was sinking lower and lower every minute. Once or twice I almost got stuck myself and this was nerve racking business, so we just left the ox to his fate, much as we regretted it.

It had rained a great deal lately and the quick-sand was more treacherous than ever. Some of the very spots traversed on the previous trip had to be avoided now, and considerable time was lost in searching for solid ground.

There was no further mishap, until we reached the steep mountain trail, where the Indian was awaiting us. He showed us the wrong trail, as we discovered, to our sorrow. It was a very narrow path, quite steep and full of rocks. When about half way up this grade one of the oxen slipped on the rocks, rolling over and almost doubling up, with his head under him. We thought he had broken his neck, but after getting him straightened out, found that he was not hurt much. The steer cut open his leg on a sharp rock and it was feared he would bleed to death. The wound was tied up with a handkerchief and after a short rest the cattle were again driven on slowly over the mountain

trail. (Oxen travel at a slow gait and should be shod when traveling over hard or rocky ground—ours were not.) The weather was now pleasant and warm and our cattle were pretty well tired out.

Every now and then one or the other would drop in his tracks from exhaustion and not get up again until he was thoroughly rested. George and I were also tired out from this long tramp in the sun, but there was no time for delay, as 3 mountains were to be crossed before we strike camp in the evening. This was accomplished however, and we retired early for a much needed long rest.

Next day the journey was continued to Clark's place where we again camped and rested. The Indian taxed us $22.00 for this trip. Part of the outfit was packed back to the Mission and stored in an old open shed—then we returned to camp, leaving the steer with the injured leg in the care of Rev. Warren, the missionary. The trail was in worse condition now than before and on three different occasions we came very near losing another ox in the mud pools. The very worst places were fixed up with brush before we dared drive the cattle over them. Once, while crossing a temporary log bridge over a narrow, but deep stream, one of the oxen stepped too close to the end of the loose logs, which tipped up, thus landing the ox in the water up to his neck, pack and all. Just the head was visible above the surface, but he floundered and splashed and snorted in his efforts to get up on the steep bank. The soil was very slippery, being clay, and every time the ox tried to take a step forward, he slipped and slid back to the water's edge. But there is always a way out of a difficulty and this time the ox found the way—he slowly crawled up that grade on his knees and when at a safe distance, got up and followed the rest of the pack.

Oct. 11.

The balance of our outfit was packed back to the Mission, when we discovered that the Indian dogs had got at some of our sacks the previous night and chewed up a considerable quantity of our bacon. We were mad enough to shoot those dogs, but dared not because the Indians were too close at hand.

The next thing to find out was to see if we could get a log hut to live in, or to build one ourselves. Mr. Rogers, the carpenter at the Mission told us that there was a deserted log cabin down at the farther end of the village, which belonged to a man in Juneau and of which he had full charge. We were told to move in and make it our home— then to write to the owner for information. The price set on it by Rogers was $50.00 but we did not care to buy, simply rent it.

The owner was never heard from however, so we were not worrying about anything. It was a roughly built log cabin, had a door, a window and bunk in it and was surrounded by 20 acres of land, all fenced in. At the northern end of this property was a fine patch of potatoes and turnips. We went to work at once, repaired the cabin, stuffed up the openings between the logs with moss and clay—then put down a board floor and our home was completed and

quite cozy. It took us just three days to repair the cabin. From the vegetable patch we secured 6 sacks of fine potatoes, which came in very handy and were stored away under the bunk. The other provisions were piled up close by the cabin and covered with canvas and tarpaulins.

Our cattle was feeding on the leaves and dry grass in the woods and what weeds could be found along the beach. The faithful ox would come to the cabin every day, poke his head and immense pair of horns inside the door and wait for his ration of potatoes, which we did not have the heart to refuse him. We decided to kill the steer (the one that caused us the most trouble) and hang up the meat in a shed to the rear of the cabin. This would give us fresh meat during the time we remained here and between that and the potatoes we were not in such a bad way after all and could save the other provisions. The Indians were busy building frame houses, the material for which was furnished by the Mission, on easy terms. To my mind this was all a waste of energy and capital, which could be applied to better advantage with our own poor people at home—for the Indian does not appreciate any favors shown him. "Once an Indian, always an Indian," as the saying goes and it fully applied here, as I discovered from personal observations during our short stay in this vicinity. So long as the Indian was left to shift for himself, live in a tent or any old shack, dress in skins and furs and live his natural life—which is to hunt and fish, eating only such foods as nature provided, he was contented and happy and well. But when they begin to adopt, or rather were forced to adopt the clothing, mode of living and food of the white man it did not agree with them, and as a natural result they developed into a race of sickly and discontented specimens of humanity. We visited a number of them here and at Chilkat and found many of them suffering with consumption and other horrible diseases.

One of these Indians had the nerve to offer us $10.00 for our ox, which cost about $75.00 landed here, but he did not get the ox.

Oct. 23-26.

Building the meat shed. It was made of small logs, nailed up securely and covered with spruce boughs to keep out the snow. On the 23d and 24th we had considerable snow, while on the 25th again it rained pretty hard. From our cabin here we have a fine view of Lynn Canal, a wide body of water, with the high mountains in the background.

The scenery is grand—off to the right some large glaciers are visible between the mountain peaks. The rising sun, shedding its beautiful reddish glow on the snow-covered mountain peaks is a magnificent sight to behold and puts one in mind of the Alps in Switzerland, as viewed from RigiKulm* at sunrise.

Nov. 1.

This day settled the fate of our troublesome steer. He was tied to a post alongside the cabin and Geo. shot him, while I stood

*Rigi-Kulm is a peak near Lake Lucerne in Switzerland.

ready with the knife to cut his throat. Then he was skinned and cut into sections and the meat hung up in our shed. This part of the work accomplished, we could now take it easy and spend some time with our neighbors, the Indians. Not one of them ever invited us to come into his house, so we called without invitation. They would send the girls around for meat every now and then and we sold it at the rate of 2 lbs. for 25 cts.

Sawing up logs for fire-wood kept us busy a good part of the time and the evenings were spent in reading over the papers which our friends and relatives sent us.

Philip King, a lumberman from Skaguay, who came to the Mission in search of timber for the saw mill, stopped with us two days. It was he who first showed us how to bake good yeast bread and before long we were quite experts at the business. For a table we used a soap box and when making biscuits a bottle served in place of a rolling pin—the rest was easy.

Nov. 8.

James Cannon, another white man, who lives with a squaw near Clark's place came to visit us. Cannon was one of the party that assisted Jack Dalton (of Dalton Trail fame) in driving some cattle inland as far as Five Finger Rapids. From him we learned how to bake bread with sour dough and it was real good. The biscuits were made in the following manner (the advice may come in handy to the reader some day). The flour was sifted into a paper we had spread over the soap box and mixed with baking-powder and a little salt. Then the water was added and the dough hastily formed. This was rolled out with the bottle and the biscuits cut out with the lid of a baking-powder can and placed into the oven in a greased pan. The biscuits were fine, for we put in baking powder enough to raise them clear out of the pan.

Nov. 12.

Herman Meyer (the butcher from Seattle, where we purchased our cattle and who also had a shop in Skaguay) called here, to look over some stray cattle. He was with us six days, waiting for a steamer to take him back home.

It was now quite cold and stormy. Steamers were behind schedule and would not run in to the Mission even if signaled. Two days ago a party of eight aboard a schooner, started out from Skaguay in a storm, bound for Dyea (6 miles around the point). The boat became unmanageable when the centre-board got out of gear and the whole outfit drifted helplessly down the canal. Two of the party became frightened and insisted on being put ashore at the first opportunity. They were landed under difficulties, the boat being in danger of smashing up in the rocks. We heard later on that these two did manage to reach Skaguay again, by travelling over the mountains which stretch along the shore. The remaining six agreed to stick to the boat and drifted with the receding tide, until at 7 o'cl. in the evening of the second day they were

fortunate enough to be carried into the harbor and landed on the beach right near our cabin. We heard their shouts of distress, rushed out with a lantern and assisted them in getting ashore. They appealed to the Rev. Warren for lodging at the Mission and he readily consented to accommodate the party as best he could.

This party also was obliged to wait here five days before a steamer heeded the signals to stop in the harbor. Every time a steamer hove in sight, it was signaled with a flag from the high flagstaff at the Mission, lights were displayed at night and the school house bell rung vigorously, but no boat would stop until the 5th day, when all got aboard and returned to Skaguay.

The days are short at this season of the year—at 1 P.M. it is dark. Our mail was brought up from Juneau on the tug *Coleman*, which make regular trips to Haines Mission, Skaguay and Dyea.

The other day Mr. Ripinsky, the storekeeper at Chilkat, gave us 3 bottles of beer, which he had recently obtained from the brewery at Juneau. We had missed the good old beer we used to get, in fact we had almost forgotten how it tasted, so this was quite a treat for us. The beer costs $5.00 per 10 gall. keg.

Nov. 14.

During the night one of our two remaining oxen either accidentally fell into a mud hole, or was driven into it by the Indians, for a certain purpose. At any rate, early in the morning, one of the Indians came over and reported that our ox was found dead. We went out to look him over and sure enough, there he was, stuck in the mud and dead as dead could be. We wished to have our breakfast first and then return for the hide, but nothing was said to the Indians. Great was our surprise when we came back and found that our ox had entirely disappeared—not a trace of him was left. The greedy Indians had cut up the body and carried the meat away to their shacks. This greatly angered us, for the hide which we intended to preserve, was no doubt entirely ruined. A search was made for the meat and hide and the greater part of it found in the house of an old Indian doctor. The latter presented a frightful sight, as he stood there, his hands and face besmeared with blood, holding the bloody knife between his teeth and grinning, like the very devil himself—but nevertheless, thoroughly frightened.

He offered all sorts of apologies trying to explain by signs and motions that the meat was bad and not fit to eat, while we tried our best to make it plain that he was entirely welcome to the meat, but had no earthly right to cut up the hide. He pretended not to understand, so finally we threatened to get the marshal from Skaguay and have him locked up. When this was explained to him, he was scared to death and could readily understand what we had previously said. (Of course, we would not go to all this trouble, but simply wanted to frighten him thoroughly and have some fun with him.) We left him abruptly and said nothing more, but we had the old fellow guessing all right.

After several days however, when he felt sure the marshal was not coming, he was very happy and always greeted us in a friendly manner—even tipping his hat. From other Indians we learned that this same fellow had served time in San Quentin prison for 7 years for practicing witchcraft. A sick squaw had appealed to him for aid and he picked out another squaw from the tribe, claiming that she had bewitched the sick one and that for this reason she must die. She was put to death and it was for this crime he served time.

Nov. 20.

Scarcely a week has passed since the ox was discovered dead in a mud-hole and last night the only one remaining died in the same manner, but in a different place. This left no doubt in our minds as to the trickery on the part of the Indians; but, in the absence of proof, there was no chance for redress. It was useless to try and get evidence, for no Indian would squeal on another one. If we could only discover the guilty one, what fun we could have with him! This time however, we warned them not to lay hands on the dead ox and our warning was heeded.

We were thoroughly disgusted with them and did not care for the hide or anything else—but to make sure that they would not touch it, we brought over a can of petroleum, cut deep gashes into the sides of the carcass and then poured in the oil, thus soaking the meat thoroughly. While this was being done, some of the old bucks watched the operation, in utter silence. Not a word was spoken—they were plainly puzzled. At last one of them ventured to ask what the fluid was and he received the curt reply, that was none of his business. Then they got excited and their actions told us that they feared it was poison, but we paid no attention to them, being satisfied with having outwitted them this time.

The job being finished in neat style, we returned to the cabin and had a good laugh over it. Not very long after, an old Indian accompanied by a younger chap, who acted as interpreter, came rushing in to the cabin and we prepared for trouble. The old fellow was all excited and demanded information in regard to the embalming fluid we had used on the ox, but he was also very promptly and forcibly informed that it was none of his affair. But he kept on talking and gesticulating in an excited manner and we understood him to say that one of his dogs had eaten some of the meat and died. This, we knew was a deliberate falsehood and he was called down for it. We were all so excited over the matter, that I expected any moment to be mixed up in a fist fight. I knew very well that George could take care of himself, but was just wondering what effect a good solar plexus blow would have on the Indian, for they are not posted at that game. However, after some further wrangling, the point was made clear to us. What he meant to say was, that his dog might eat the meat and die from the effects of the supposed poison. We could not help laughing then, in spite of all the excitement. Thinking the joke had been carried far enough, I told him what the fluid was—but he would not

believe it until he was permitted to smell of the empty can and then he walked away, perfectly satisfied.

It was well that he did get the information, for if by chance one of his dogs had died, we would certainly be blamed for it. Then he would very likely demand a cash sum, or its equivalent in blankets. (The latter are good in stock in trade. They buy up a squaw for a certain number of blankets and perhaps a money consideration besides.) We feared that our little joke might cause trouble and were always on the alert, when any of the Indians were around, but nothing ever came of it. For all we know, they may have eaten the meat, as they did eat the previous lot.

A short time ago, the Chilkats* (as this tribe is called) held a big feast called "Potlatch," in Yindistucka, the little village, 3 miles up the river. They feasted in great style, sang, danced and shouted all day and night long. Each Indian brought presents for his relatives and friends—such as blankets, clothing, money, etc. White men were only permitted to witness the celebration, if they came well provided with presents—but even then they were not welcome guests. We thought it wise to stay away, on account of our little joke and the trick we had played on Co-to-wah. The Indians were highly excited during the three or four days the feast lasted.

Co-to-wah, we were told, was bound to outdo his predecessor in generosity, so as to make himself more popular with the tribe. He gave away a good many blankets and also cash money. He is known to be in

---

*The Chilkats lived along the western arm of Lynn Canal.

comfortable circumstances financially, since his contract with the Alaska Packer's Ass'n. yields him a good profit, he having the entire deal in hand and making his own terms with the tribe. Each band has its own chief and while trading with one another, no tribe can come into the other one's territory and do business there, without paying tribute. The longer we are among these Indians, the better we learn their tricky ways. They are shrewd—always waiting for a chance to get the best of a white man, whom they dislike. Being filthy in the mode of living and habits, utterly disregarding all proper care of the body, many are sufferers of the most loathsome diseases. They are not quarrelsome, unless wronged in some way and they fear the law; because, as a rule, severe sentence is meted out to them, if found guilty of committing a crime.

An old Indian guide, living here, calls himself "Schwatka" and claims to have served as a guide with Lieut. Schwatka, when the latter was out on a surveying trip in Alaska, for the U.S. government.* He is the brother of the old Indian doctor and a shrewd, but jolly good fellow. He has asked us a number of times, "You go Klonedick?" (Klondike). When assured that the Klondike region was our destination, he answered quickly, "Klonedick, 2 $^{1}/_{2}$ moon, I go"— meaning possibly 2 $^{1}/_{2}$ months later he would go. (To make plain the 2 $^{1}/_{2}$ months, he held up 2 fingers and placed his forefinger over the two and the total was 2 $^{1}/_{2}$.)

Strange to say, in this case "moon" meant month, while the old Indian at Aqualtu used the same expression, in stating his age ("90 moons"—meaning years).

The other day we met Schwatka and the old doctor again and demanded a cash sum for the hide which the latter had ruined. They kept on talking about "meat, no good," while we tried our best to explain that we wanted the money for the hide and not the meat. Both walked away finally, but it was not 10 minutes later, when they brought us the hide of the last ox we lost, whose carcass was soaked with kerosene, and carried it inside the enclosure. They were told that this was not the hide we had reference to and to take it back home and bring us the money, or have the Marshal sent after them, when we get to Skaguay.

All was plain to them now and Schwatka was mad clean through, while the doctor had a scared look. (He was probably thinking of San Quentin prison.) These Indians seldom greet a white man, but Schwatka and his brother were the exception. They all have peculiar names, such as Johnson, Isaacs, Mr. Charles, Joe, etc.

There are now 3 stores at Chilkat— Ripinsky's, Koehler and James' and Gibsons'. Jack Dalton lives in a comfortable frame house here, when not engaged in taking pack trains into the interior. Wm. Dickinson, a half breed Indian also lives in Chilkat. He is an educated man and seemed to hold the position of general advisor to the tribe.

*Lieutenant Frederick Schwatka led an 1883 expedition that was the first to follow the Yukon River in its entirety.

Dec. 4.

The weather is cold and it has snowed considerable lately. I made a trip to Skaguay is search of the owner of the stranded schooner, *Cape Pigeon*, which was still on the beach at Haines Mission. We intended to hire this boat and take our outfit to Skaguay or Dyea, preparatory to the inland trip. The owner was readily found—he, as well as the former owner, Capt. Morton, from Maine, came back to the Mission with me and all four took a hand at repairing the damaged boat. Along about this time the Rev. Warren paid us a visit, stating that he had no water in his house and all the pipes leading from the school to the house (a distance of about 100 ft.) were frozen. He wanted our assistance in digging up the pipes and setting them lower in the ground, offering $3.00 per day ea. for our services. We could not very well refuse on account of his previous kindness, although well aware of the fact that the Indians refused to work for less than $4.00. (A pretty example of the Indian's appreciation of all that is done for him by the Missionary.) So we started work with pick and shovel, but soon found out that it was an awful task. The ground was frozen solid and hard as rock, breaking off in little chips, like glass.

I stuck to it for 3 days, when my wrist began to swell up and pain me—so I was obliged to quit. Geo. kept at it for another day, when he too gave it up for a tough proposition. Mr. Warren paid us for our work and then gave the Indians a chance to show what they could do. We did not remain at the Mission long enough to see the result of their work.

Dyea and the Chilkoot Pass

Chapter Three

Dec. 17.

TODAY OUR OUTFIT was packed aboard the schooner and after bidding our friends a last farewell, we started up the canal at 7 A.M. bound for Skaguay. Mr. Warren had promised to forward our mail. It was a cool, but clear day and for the last time we had opportunity to see the sun's first rays settling on the snow-covered mountain peaks—a sight never to be forgotten!

New surroundings, a new life and perhaps, misfortune await us, but we will reach the point of our destination (Stewart River) if such a thing be possible. A slight breeze favored us and the boat sailed along over the ruffled water at a moderate pace, until noon, when we were obliged to use the long oars. This was very tiresome work, but one soon becomes accustomed to most anything, if the good will is there and so it was in this case. Shortly after noon it grew quite warm and we enjoyed the trip immensely. At 2 P.M. a head wind was encountered, sweeping down from the mountains and along the canal. Slow progress was made until 5 o'cl. when the breeze was again in our favor and we were glad of the opportunity to put aside the heavy oars; but our joy was of but short duration—for hardly ½ hour had passed before we were again becalmed. We rowed away slowly, but steadily, until 7 o'cl. when the lights of Skaguay were sighted and at 7:30 we had landed and tied the boat up at one of the wharves. (There were 3 of these—and all put up since our previous visit, in September.) Everyone advised us to take the Dyea trail and cross the coast mountains via Chilcoot Pass. It was not safe to risk a trip to Dyea tonight (6 miles beyond) so Geo. and myself secured lodging at the "Gem Hotel," where we had a fairly good bed for 50 cts. each. (By fairly good bed I mean an ordinary bunk, with mattress and blanket.) Next day the weather was altogether too stormy for a trip in a small schooner, and we could not leave here until the 19th (Sunday). We arrived at Dyea about noon when the tide was on the ebb and had our goods landed on the mud flat. A time was then hired to haul the outfit up the road two miles, just beyond Dyea, where we found good camping ground in the woods. The tent was pitched near an old log house

MAIN STREET OF DYEA, TAKEN FROM THE BEACH

JOSEPH T. FIELD'S FORMER STORE, OUR HOME AT DYEA FROM DECEMBER 22, 1897 TO JANUARY 14, 1898

NEW ARRIVALS CAMPED BEYOND DYEA, JANUARY 1898

(formerly Field's* store) which was at this time occupied by Doc McCormack, of San Francisco.

We soon felt quite at home again, although not quite as comfortable as in our log cabin at the Mission. From now on however, the tent must be our shelter and home. For the following three days the weather was very disagreeable, changing from snow to rain.

Pack-trains of horses and mules were passing up and down the trail, carrying the outfits of the gold-hunters. A number of teams were also engaged in hauling goods on wagons. The charges for hauling from "Dyea" to "Canyon City" (10 miles) were 1 cts. per lb.; Canyon City to "Sheep Camp" (4 miles up the canyon), 7 cts.; Sheep Camp to "The Scales" (3 ½ miles—2 miles of packing), 5 cts.; and from

*Joseph T. Field.

Scales to summit (½ mile packing), 1¼ cts.

Canyon City derives its name from the location at mouth of canyon. Sheep Camp is so named because the hunters of mountain sheep were in the habit of camping in this particular locality—it is also the timber line, and The Scales was the place where packers weighed their packs, before commencing the steep ascent to the Summit.

Our stock of provisions had to be replenished, so I made the trip to Skaguay, spending two days there, in selecting a new supply. Upon my return, Doc McCormack was kind enough to permit us to store the entire outfit in his cabin and reserved two bunks for us to sleep in. In return for this kindness we sawed up and chopped all of Doc's supply of logs, for firewood. Christmas Day was like any other day to us—only we longed to be with the Dear Ones left behind. The entire day was spent in sawing up logs. In the evening Doc invited us to a supper consisting of brown beans, salt pork and beef and then we sat around the fire until after midnight, telling stories. Doc also set up the cigars, which were considered quite a treat, since we always smoked a pipe.

New Years found us still at work, sawing up Doc's logs. We had left orders at Skaguay to have our mail forwarded to Dyea, but for some reason or other it had been delayed, so I decided to go over after it. A party of six started out on a cold and stormy day, in an open Columbia River sailboat. The waves were choppy and there was a stiff headwind on. In order to make any headway at all, it was necessary to take short tacks and when out some distance, the waves began to roll dangerously high, pitching and rolling our boat around until we began to wish we had remained on solid land. We all sat in the bottom of the boat, almost numb with cold, the spray dashing over us continually. The trip lasted just 2 ¹/₂ hours and when we landed I was compelled to enter an eating-house near by and thaw out by the fire before I could reach in my pocket for the fare of $1.00. It was my worst experience on a sailboat. In fair wind and weather the run is made in ³/₄ hrs. I wanted no more sailing that day, so after procuring the mail, my lodging was secured and next day I returned to Dyea.

Jan. 1898.

The trail being in fair condition, we took advantage of the opportunity and hauled our first load of 300 lbs. each, on sleds, to Finnegan's Point* (6 miles beyond). The trail winds along Dyea River is a perfectly level stretch, as far as the Point. While there was hardly enough snow for good sledding, we continued to haul one load each day.

The goods are left beside the trail and simply covered with canvas or tarpaulin, to protect them from the snow or rain. There is no danger of them being stolen, because it is worth your life up in this country to take anything not belonging to you. As water in the river is very low at this season of the year, we crossed to the opposite bank, by sliding the sleds over logs. There were 4 or 5 crossings like this and in some places along the trail there were rocks. It was a hard pull then and we always doubled up, one assisting the other.

Jan. 11.

This evening there was a heavy fall of snow, which improved conditions. We tried to buy a small box in one of the [Dyea] stores, to pack some goods in, but found boxes a very scarce article. Lumber is scarce at $40.00 per M, so the boxes came in handy for shelving, counters, etc.

The town is full of dogs and sometimes during the night, they set up a fearful howling, keeping us awake. It is one long, drawn-out howl, starting at a low note and ending in a higher pitch. One that has never heard the howling of a pack of Alaskan dogs has no conception of this hideous, soul-piercing music.

An enterprising young chap started a dog hospital where the canines are cared for and fed for $10.00 per month. He had about 50 of them in his care at this time. The dogs were fed on corn-meal principally. A number of miners from the interior arrived here with dog teams and spoke favorably of the gold country.

FINNEGAN'S POINT, SIX MILES BEYOND DYEA

---

*Finnegan's Point, five to six miles from Dyea, consisted of a saloon, restaurant, and blacksmith shop. Pat Finnegan and his sons for a time charged a toll of $2 per horse for using their bridge, until they were overwhelmed by the masses of miners who simply passed by without paying.

CANYON CITY, TEN MILES FROM DYEA, CONSISTS OF A FEW STORES AND A NUMBER OF SALOONS

MOUTH OF THE CANYON, TAKEN FROM CANYON CITY

Jan. 14.

Today our last load was hauled to the Point. It was a big one, including the bulky camp outfit—tent, poles, kettles, etc. We had placed our goods inside an old log cabin the other day, but were now asked by the owner to remove some to another cabin, as the former was just sold. Our next haul was from Finnegan's Point to Canyon City, a distance of 4 miles. After a rest of one day, we started in on this work. Each hauled 2 loads a day (of 250 lbs. each) covering 16 miles in the two round trips. The thermometer registered 35 degrees—pleasant weather. Canyon City is a little village, consisting of a few stores and a number of saloons. Beer, whiskey or cigars cost 25 cts. Our goods are cached right in the mouth of the canyon, beside a high bluff. Dyea River runs down this canyon, but at this season of the year it is frozen up pretty solid. A party coming out from "30 Mile River," reported that he experienced no very cold weather at any time during his trip. A little later on another party told us it was 10 to 15 below at Dawson City, which gave us a chill.

Jan. 18.

The weather was cold today, with a strong headwind blowing from the north. Snow is heaped up in big drifts on the trail, but we succeeded in making our customary two trips—yesterday the same.

Jan. 19.

During the night 4 in. of snow fell. Our camp outfit was hauled to the canyon and the tent pitched on the ice. Then we scattered spruce boughs over the floor and spread out our sleeping bags on top of them. We managed to keep warm nights by crawling into the sleeping-bags with our clothes on and covering up with blankets. Our meals are always cooked on the stove. Beans were on the bill of fare two and three times a day—the other dishes were oatmeal, rice, bacon, cornmeal, pan-cakes, dried fruit and bread. The bill of fare was changed from time to time, but beans were generally served twice a day, for a leader. Up on Chilkat River one day we foolishly cooked some dried apples in a galvanized iron bucket and both of us were deathly sick for a time. But experience is the best teacher, as the saying goes—after that all fruit was cooked in enameled pots. We were fast becoming quite expert at cooking and could flop a pan-cake in fine style. How good everything we ate tasted—and it was only because we were always hungry and working hard.

Jan. 20.

Both of us returned to Dyea for mail and waited in vain until the 22d—still no mail in sight, so we returned to camp.

Jan. 23.

The next camping ground and the last one this side of the coast mountains, is Sheep Camp (4 miles up the Canyon). Each hauled 2 loads of 200 lbs. each and every day. The first mile of the trip is slightly up grade, with ups and downs and a few steep grades. After emerging from the canyon, we pass Camp Pleasant (1 $^1/_2$ miles). Above that point there is a slight, but steady upgrade, all the way to Sheep Camp. The latter is quite a lively place—everybody camped here, because there is no timber beyond. The whole space is occupied by tents, frame-houses, stores and saloons. Work on the overhead cable road was being rushed and the system will soon be in operation. It was built for the purpose of hauling freight from Canyon City to the summit. There was a power house at Canyon City, one at Sheep Camp and another on the summit. The cable is stretched on poles and goods are carried in specially constructed iron boxes which run on a wheel along the cable.

CAMP PLEASANT

Jan. 24.

During the night it rained some. We have [a] great spot, coasting down the canyon on our return trips. I had a narrow escape from colliding with a team one day, which unexpectedly appeared around a sharp turn in the trail—but managed to steer off to one side, dashing head first into a bank of snow, not the least bit hurt. One day I was pulling Geo. along on the sled and when we reached a steep down grade I lost all control of the sled and Geo. sailed down like a streak, plunging into a snow-bank and landing squarely over a large opening in the ice. He barely missed falling through to the water below.

BIRD'S EYE VIEW OF SHEEP CAMP, TAKEN FROM THE HILL BEYOND

THE BUSINESS
SECTION OF
SHEEP CAMP

OUR CAMP AT SHEEP
CAMP, JANUARY 30
TO APRIL 6, 1898

Jan. 25-29.

One load a-piece was hauled these four days. It was disagreeable weather—snowing and raining by turns. On the 29th just a light load was hauled and next day we took up the camp outfit and pitched our tent on the side of a hill, where the snow was 7 ft. deep. There was no chance to drive stakes, so we levelled off a large space, set up our upright poles and fastened the sides and ends of the tent to heavy logs. Next a frame was built over the tent, made from stout branches and the whole thing covered with spruce boughs, to keep the snow from falling on our tent. The real Winter had not set in yet—colder weather was coming. On the 31st we returned to Dyea for mail. The distance of 14 miles was covered in 3 hours flat—pulling a sled on which we carried our sleeping-bags and some provisions. When in Dyea, Doc's cabin was our home. It was bitter cold weather, but we rather enjoyed this little vacation. No mail was found at Dyea so I again made the trip to Skaguay. There was no mail for either of us and I returned to Dyea in disgust. We hunted up our old friend Meyer, who ran a butcher shop in Dyea and to our surprise found he had a whole box full of papers and letters he had saved for us, knowing that sooner or later he would meet us in Dyea. Among the lot there were letters from our relatives and friends, besides a big bundle of newspapers, which we eagerly read over, so as to ascertain the latest news (about 2 weeks after issue).

Feb. 2.

The weather was very cold today and I very nearly froze my fingers on the way back to Sheep Camp. The cold continued for the following three days, so we did not venture out over the trail.

Feb. 6.

Today Geo. and I made a trip to "Stone House"* (a cluster of rocks 1 ½ miles above Sheep Camp). I carried a Kodak camera, which my brother in Milwaukee had forwarded to me at the Mission, after we had returned there from our disastrous trip over the Dalton Trail with the oxen. Geo. was posing at the rocks for just a minute and

*From Sheep Camp, the trail rose very sharply. Stone House—a huge overhanging boulder—provided one of the few places where a climber could rest.

had one of his cheeks frozen—but he was not aware of this until a party passing by called his attention to it. Everything we cook freezes up during the night and the water in our buckets is always frozen solid. It took us some little time to find out just what quantity of beans it takes to fill the pot, after they are boiled, for they swell up to 3 times their natural size. But we were becoming more expert at cooking every day and soon found out that the beans should be soaked in water before they are boiled.

Feb. 9.

Wishing to take a look at the famous Chilcoot Pass (4 miles above here) I started out this morning, with a pair of slippery shoepacks on my feet, instead of the moccasins, which are more appropriate in dry weather. My camera was carried under the arm. When I reached The Scales and looked up that steep grade leading to Chilcoot Pass, I wondered if it was possible for me to undertake the trip without the aid of a stick. Not a speck of timber can be found here—not even shrubbery, Sheep Camp being the last timber ground this side of the coast range. At least 100 men were constantly in line on that grade, with packs on their backs, all working hard to get their outfits over the mountains. I started up boldly, taking good care not to lose my camera. There was a rope stretched from Scales to Summit, and I hugged that rope pretty closely all the way up that steep grade of 600 ft. All around us, as far the eye could reach, was snow and ice and the only foot holds were

the holes stamped in the snow by this steady line of men climbing up the mountain. There were a number of benches dug into the snow on one side of the trail, where the weary packers had a chance to sit down and rest.

The first time I stepped out of line to regain my wind, it made me dizzy to look down that awful grade so I did not linger long, but kept my eyes fixed on the Summit, trying hard to forget what was behind and below me. The packs carried up ranged all the way from 50 to 125 lbs. After reaching the top of this climb, I stopped to view the surrounding scenery. It was a pretty site and one never to be forgotten. Wherever the eye rested, there were the mountain peaks, all covered with snow. But one realizes at once that this is no place for play and the only way to get an outfit on the Summit is to simply keep at it until the feat is accomplished, unless one cared to pay the exorbitant rates charged by a party named Burns* who operated the sled cable-road. The power was furnished by horses at The Scales. A great

GEORGE HARTMANN SAWING LOGS FOR FIREWOOD AT SHEEP CAMP

*By December 1897, Archie Burns operated the first crude tramway over Chilkoot Pass—an endless rope wound around a wheel, turned by horses moving in a circle. By May there were at least five tramways operating, most on a much larger scale. But few miners could afford them.

many of the outfits belonging to parties who had failed to cross the mountains the years previous, were found scattered all over the Pass. Long poles, with rags tied to them, indicated the places where the various outfits were located—but at this time everything was covered with snow, anywhere from 10 to 20 feet deep. We observed several parties digging up their outfits and they certainly had a hard time of it. The Canadian North-West Mounted Police had established headquarters in the Pass and collected duty on all the outfits.

It was time for me to start out on the return trip, which, as I soon found out, was no easy matter. I got safely down the first grade, but just as I reached the edge of the 600 ft. grade, my feet slipped from under me, and the next instant I was sliding down hill at such a rapid pace, it made my hair stand on end. I could fancy myself sailing through space and landing on top of the power-house below. My situation was anything but a pleasant one. Having no stick with which to check the speed, there was but one chance for me, and that was to dig my shoes into the soft snow, on either side of the slide. So with a mighty effort I finally accomplished this feat and came to a sudden halt. The camera was still with me for I hung on to it, come what may.

For a few moments I studied over the situation, when a fellow coming down the slide at a rapid pace shouted for me to get out of the way and brought me to my senses. A collision was imminent, so without further reflection I rolled over to one side into the deep snow, just as the other fellow sailed by. It was a close shave and sliding had no further attraction for me. Moving by inches, over to where the rope was, I made the descent without further mishap and returned to camp, where we had a good laugh over my hair-raising experience. Along about this time a number of people had parts of their outfit stolen, but the guilty ones could not be detected. A committee was appointed at Sheep Camp to investigate the matter. All the tents along the trail were searched, with the result that a considerable quantity of the stolen goods were found in the tent of three fellows who happened to be short of provisions and simply stole from others. Sacks were found bearing the names of other parties and no further evidence was required. The committee waited for their return to camp, caught the three of them and marched them down to Sheep Camp for trial.* It did not take long to appoint judge and jury in this case. The prisoners were given a hearing in one of the large tents along the main trail. One of the trio proved

---

*The trial of three men—Wellington, Dean, and Hansen—was held in a tent. Dean, who had only recently joined the other two, was freed. Wellington and Hansen were found guilty. Wellington, according to a slightly different version than Shape's story, broke from his captors, took out a hidden pistol, cut a hole in the tent with a knife, and ran down the trail. As the leading man in pursuit chased him, Wellington shot himself. Hansen, after the trial reconvened, was sentenced to fifty lashes.

himself innocent and was promptly discharged, the other two were guilty. The sentence meted out to number one was a severe flogging. He was stripped, tied to a post out on the trail, in broad day-light and received a number of lashes over his bare back, before a crowd of jeering and threatening people. It had not been decided what to do with number two, but excitement ran high and a great many favored lynching—he fully deserved it.

About 8 P.M. when we were sitting in our tent, reading papers, an awful shout startled us. It was not the shout of an angry mob, but the shout of a single man, fighting for his life and crying out in wild dispair. It was almost immediately followed by two pistol shots, fired in rapid succession. We realized at once that something unusual had happened and thought of the prisoner. Rushing down to the trail, we were warned to keep back, for fear of further shooting. However, after waiting a few minutes, all was quiet and we advanced down the trail. Soon we came upon a crowd of men surrounding the lifeless body of a man. There he lay in the snow, with a bullet hole in his forehead—dead. It was the prisoner. Some said that he attempted to escape and failing, committed suicide. The strange thing about it was the fact that he had a belt full of cartridges strapped over his coat, and the revolver lay at his side. Surely the man while on trial was not permitted to be armed in this fashion. However, I did not attend the trial and cannot say how it happened. It was generally understood that he was condemned to be shot and no questions were

asked. Both of these fellows deserved what punishment they received—for any man who would steal another's food up in this country is the lowest kind of criminal. There are no corner grocery stores here, where one can buy food at any time, even if he had the necessary funds. Number one, after being flogged, was marched back to Dyea by members of the committee, wearing a placard marked "Thief—push him along." We saw him coming down the trail, grinning and smoking a pipe as unconcerned as if nothing had happened. At Dyea he was placed aboard a steamer and warned, as he valued his life, never to show his face on the Dyea trail again. The news of the shooting soon spread to Dyea and next day the marshal came to investigate the matter. But nothing ever came of it, since the guilty ones, if such they were, had already fled over the summit. After that there was no more stealing along the Dyea trail.

Feb. 11.

We started out today with a load of 220 lbs. on our sled and hauled it up the steep grades, to Stone House; discarded 70 lbs. here and hauled the balance to The Scales. But the grades above Stone House are too steep for sleds, so we shall haul our goods as far as Stone House and then pack them to The Scales and later on, to the Summit (Chilcoot Pass) always returning to Sheep Camp when our day's labor is finished.

Feb. 12.

This day we hauled 600 lbs., in 3 trips, to Stone

House (it takes 2 ¹/₂ hrs. for the round trip of 3 miles, on account of the steep grades).

STONE HOUSE

Feb. 13.

The weather being too stormy, only 200 lbs. were hauled.

Feb. 14.

Still stormy and cold, but we hauled 400 lbs.

Feb. 15.

Very severe weather—we could not venture out.

Feb. 16.

We are again longing for news from home—so I started out on the 14 mile jaunt to Dyea, Geo. remaining at Sheep Camp. To my great surprise I was rewarded with a letter from Mr. O. (one of our former party, who backed out in Seattle) and Col. Wilson, an acquaintance, from New York. The letter stated that they were both at Dyea, living with Doc Robey and intended to join our party on the trip inland to Stewart River; but nothing ever came of it and later on both returned to the states. (Col. Wilson was far too stout a man to climb over the summit, not to say anything of carrying a pack and the other fellow was too big a coward.)

The cold spell (18 below) lasted until the 23rd when I returned to Sheep Camp with Col. Wilson. Doc Robey's quarters at Dyea were very uncomfortable and cold. A board bench and 2 blankets constituted the bed and I retired at night with all my clothes on—cap, mittens, moccasins, coat and all. Sound sleep was out of the question, on account of the extreme cold. In the middle of the night, one of the party would get out and start a fire in the little stove and all hands squatted around some, to keep from freezing. It was the only time I suffered intensely from the cold.

Feb. 24-25.

Weather too cold and stormy to venture out.

Feb. 26.

The weather has moderated—it is snowing and raining by turns. My partner Geo. and the Col. returned to Dyea.

Feb. 27.

After gathering in a lot of firewood, I tried my hand at bread-baking, with a sour dough. The two loaves I pulled out of that oven were real beauties and I felt very proud over the results.

Feb. 28.

Weather again cold and stormy—hauled 300 lbs. in three trips. The trail was lined with sleds drawn by horses, dogs, oxen and mules. One man from Seattle even had an elk drawing his load. Off in the distance, to the left of the trail there was a big glacier, apparently hanging over the edge of the mountain. It was composed of one solid mass of ice, of a pale green color. This afternoon while engaged in hauling my sled to Stone House, I was startled by what sounded like the report of a cannon, fired at some distance. Looking up at the mountain, from whence came the disturbance, the sight I beheld glued me to the spot. The immense glacier of ice had bursted and the huge mass came tearing down the mountain side, with a roar like thunder. A great cloud, like dust, arose from the mountain top and I watched the thrilling spectacle, until the last chunk of ice had lodged in the valley below. It was a sight never to be forgotten and I felt amply rewarded for all the hard work thus far performed, even if I should see nothing more of this grand wild country.

Mar. 1.

Stormy weather, but I hauled 200 lbs. in two trips. The fact that today was my birthday never occurred to me, until Geo. upon his return from Dyea with Mr. O. put me in mind of it.

Mar. 2.

Today we hauled 400 lbs. each in 2 trips. Mr. O. accompanied us and when he took a look at the high climb to the summit and began to realize what a tough proposition it really was, he suddenly lost all enthusiasm

for the trip and preferred to return to home and mamma. As far as the Colonel was concerned, that individual was far too corpulent to make the ascent.

Mar. 3.

Hauled 100 lbs. this morning and Geo. packed 50 lbs. (a horse had stepped on and damaged Geo.'s sled yesterday and is being repaired). In the afternoon we hauled 200 lbs. together, intending also to do some packing from Stone House to Scales, but severe weather prevented this. By evening however, it was again mild and pleasant. (This gives an idea of the sudden changes of temperature.) I enjoyed a good hearty laugh today, over an old man who was hauling a heavy load over the trail. He had his wife and little daughter with him:

INDIANS RETURNING FROM CHILKOOT PASS, HAVING LOST ONE MOTHER AND CHILD IN A BLIZZARD. PHOTO TAKEN AT SHEEP CAMP.

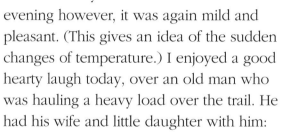

ELK HAULING THE LOADED SLED OF H.H. SMITH OF SEATTLE PAST STONE HOUSE

When I passed him, he turned to me with a look of despair overspreading his features and said: "God Almighty keeps his gold in a mighty safe place, don't he?" I could not help roaring at this remark, although I fully agreed with him. All of our outfit is now at Stone House, excepting the tent and cooking utensils. We are up before 6 in the morning and after breakfast get to work at once. Kindling wood is always prepared ready for use, so there will be no delay in getting warmed up and cooking the supper, when we return late in the afternoon. The hard work makes us perspire freely, in spite of the cold weather—therefore it is unsafe to stand still, even for just a few minutes, because you get chilled to the bone. On the return trip we always ran down the steep grade.

Mar. 4.

More snow for a change, with south wind. Packed 45, 50 and 75 lbs. each, from Stone House to Scales, in 3 trips. (Distance 2 miles.) Packing 50 lbs. on your back is hard work also—but I would rather pack it up a steep grade than try to haul it up on a sled. The 75 lb. pack was a big load for new beginners, but we managed to land it. When tired out, we rest our backs by setting the packs on some snow-bank and sitting down for a few moments—or, sometimes we rest it on a stack of provisions, which are scattered all along the trail, but never is the pack unstrapped. A 2 mile tramp, up steep grades, with 50 lbs. on your back, is no picnic, especially as you are compelled to walk in a stooping position. If the pack is not adjusted properly, so it sets well up on your back it will feel like 200 lbs. before you cover half the distance. This evening we have a little rain, just for variety.

Mar. 5.

Packed 320 lbs. together, in 3 trips. A strong wind blowing from the south was of great benefit to us in climbing the grades.

The water is very bad and most everybody is suffering from dysentery. They say the water is contaminated with the carcasses of horses, which died along the trail last summer.

Mar. 6.

The weather is clear and warm—we packed 396 lbs. in 3 trips. Being pretty well hardened to the work by this time, we can carry a pack as well as any of them. With 2 pair of heavy German socks on and wearing moccasins (in dry weather) we manage to keep our feet warm. In wet weather the arctics come in handy.

Mar. 7.

Heavy snow-storm—nothing done. We pass away the time sawing firewood or reading papers and smoking a pipe. Sitting in a tent all day long is anything but pleasant, especially when you have a partner who is not communicative and continually worrying over the outcome of the trip.

Mar. 8.

Still snowing, but much milder weather. Packed 401 lbs. in 4 trips, today. The total distance covered was 19 miles. Leaving Sheep Camp at 7 A.M. we walked 1 ¹/₂ miles to Stone House, carried 4 packs from Stone House to Scales (2 miles) and returned to Sheep Camp by 5 P.M.

Mar. 9.

Returned to Dyea and Skaguay for mail. The charges for delivering to Sheep Camp were 10 cts. per letter, but no mail was received for some time. I waited in vain, until the 14th, and then returned to camp. Geo. in the mean time packing goods to The Scales.

Mar. 15.

Made 3 trips to The Scales.

Mar. 16.

Hauled 110 lbs. together, to The Scales and carried 3 packs from Scales to Summit. It was a fine, clear day and quite warm. At least 150 men were continually in line on the steep climb to the summit—carrying packs of 25 to 125 lbs. and all in a hurry to get their goods over the mountains. Very few walked down on the return trip—that was too slow a process. Coming down, we walked around one of the peaks, over what is called the Peterson trail, to where the slides were and then slid down, all the way to The Scales, which was fine sport. (Of course everyone had an extra thick layer of canvas sewed on the seat of his overalls.) Grooves 5 and 6 feet deep were worn into the snow, where we slid down; there was no chance to look to right or left. All we had to be careful about was not to run into those ahead of us. The speed was checked by crossing the legs and holding one foot out straight, ready to push it against the side of the groove, or by extending the elbows in like manner.

CLIMBING THE SUMMIT WITH OUR PACKS, OUR GOODS IN THE FOREGROUND. TWELVE DAYS WORK.

Mar. 17.

Good weather. Carried one pack from Stone House to Scales and made 5 trips to the Summit (one of the packs weighing 75 lbs.). We are not neglecting an opportunity to put in a good day's work.

Mar. 18.

Cold and stormy—but made 5 trips to Summit. One could not linger long in the Pass, for the cold, biting wind was something terrific. Sometimes the weather is warm and pleasant on the way up, but before our packs were deposited with the other goods, a storm would spring up very suddenly and then it was a case of hustle to get back to

PULLING A HORSE UP
THE SUMMIT, OVER
PETERSON TRAIL

The Scales. When such a storm comes up one must put on mittens and cover up face and ears at once; the change from warm to freezing cold is so sudden and penetrating.

Mar. 19.

Pleasant weather. Made 4 trips to Summit. We carry with us in the morning a lunch, consisting of hard tack and bacon, previously fried and that is washed down with ice water.

Mar. 20.

Rested, today—not feeling well.

Mar. 21.

Weather very stormy. Packed one bag of clothing from Sheep Camp to Summit. It was bitter cold.

GEORGE HARTMANN
ON CHILKOOT PASS

Mar. 22.

Snow storm raging—could not risk a trip to Summit.

Mar. 23-24.

Made 5 trips to Summit each day.

Mar. 25-31.

Went to Dyea for mail and returned on the 31st. Dyea was no longer the bustling little town of three months ago—everybody is up above here, piling goods over the Summit. I found Col. Wilson (who by the way is an old actor) singing in one of the dance halls, at a salary of $50.00 per week and Mr. O. was one of the cappers in the gambling department of this institution. (Just for pastime as he explained to me.) On the 29th they had a heavy rainstorm at Dyea.

Apr. 1.

Very stormy weather prevented the moving of our camp outfit over the Summit and on down to Lake Lindemann, the next camping ground (10 miles from Summit).

Apr. 2.

The storm is still raging fiercely above here and we dared not venture over the trail.

Apr. 3.

Some of the foolhardy ones did go out in the storm and this morning something like 50 or

60 lost their lives in a big snowslide just above Stone House.* The mild weather we had of late loosened up the snow on the mountains, and without warning it came sliding down the slope, on both sides of the gulch, packing tighter as it rushed along, until the bottom was reached and there it was piled up 20 to 30 ft. deep. The unfortunate men caught in this trap had no show for their lives. Blinded by snow, they were not aware of their danger until it was too late and this vast mass of snow piled on top of them.

Apr. 4.

The trail is blocked with sleds and teams. Several hundred men are engaged in digging up the bodies. Our camping outfit was hauled over the trail, but no one with a pack was permitted to pass the scene of this recent disaster; so the tent and other material was cached near by and we returned to Sheep Camp, stopping with a friend there. It was a gruesome sight, to see 15 or 20 dead bodies arranged in a line on the snow, just as they were found, frozen stiff; some with arms extended, others with legs drawn up, showing they made their death struggle under the snow. Our entire outfit, excepting tent and cooking utensils, is now on the Summit and we are anxious to move on to Lake Lindemann.

---

*As long as winter conditions prevailed, the pass remained in fairly good condition. But the late storm Shape notes added to the snowpack and, during the heat of the day, avalanches and snow slides occurred. Stampeders were urged to pack at night when the trail was frozen, but many ignored the advice. On April 3, tons of wet snow gave way and buried hundreds of stampeders. Most were able to claw their way out, and frantic rescue efforts saved others. Still, fifty-six died and were buried at the Slide Cemetery on the trail near Dyea.

Apr. 5.

Arose at 5 A.M. and packed our goods beyond the forbidden ground, before any of the guards were on duty there. Then we moved up to the Summit, where we discovered our goods were covered up with snow, from 8 to 10 ft. deep. The first thing to be done now was to dig up the outfit and place it on high ground. This required considerable time. Then the duty on our goods had to be paid, for the Canadian Customs officials had moved their headquarters from Lake Bennett to Chilcoot Pass. We paid $47.25 and thereby hangs a tale. Everyone was requested to produce bills, covering the goods in the outfit. We had something like 35 or 3600 lbs. all told, but the bills covered only 2300 lbs. A party advised us to place a $5.00 note between the bills, when we see the customs broker. We did so and were fixed up in short order, passing on to the inspector, who had his headquarters in a log cabin, next door. Here the duty was paid and a receipt given for the money. No attempt was made to inspect the goods, this being utterly impossible, for the whole pass was strewn with hundreds of tons of goods. It was now too late to make Lake Lindemann, so we again returned to our friend in Sheep Camp.

CANADIAN CUSTOM HOUSE ON THE SUMMIT. CROSSED THE SUMMIT APRIL 6, 1898.

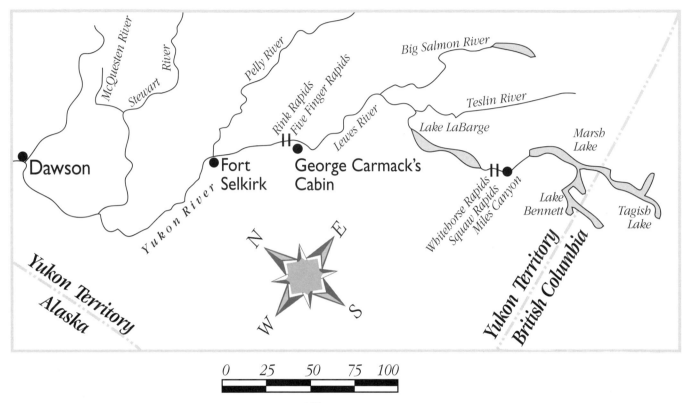

Lake Lindeman to McQuesten River

Chapter Four

Apr. 6.

AROSE AT 4:30 left Sheep Camp 5:30 and the Summit at 9 o'clock, with our camp outfit and sled. It was a long run to Lindemann—arrived there at 3 P.M. Our tent was pitched on the shore, $^1/_2$ mile below the town of Lindemann (which lies at the head of the lake.) Lindemann is the head of navigation. Timber being scarce here, we decided to move on to L[ake] Bennett, a little later, and build a boat there. The lake is frozen over and covered with snow—one would not know there was a lake there, only for the formation of the mountains along shore and the water holes in the ice, from which water is dipped by means of a bucket. This is the first timber ground beyond the Summit.

The tramp to Lindemann was a long one and tiresome. After leaving the Summit, we started down a very steep grade, which leads to Crater Lake. Then comes a level stretch, with just a few grades; next Long Lake and Deep Lake. The trail leading to these lakes winds its course in the mountain passes, which are filled with snow—nothing but snow and ice up here. After passing Deep Lake we come to the canyon and this leads us to Lindemann. In this canyon are some mighty steep grades and it is very difficult to manage a loaded sled. The latter is rigged up with a gee-pole and before going down the steepest grades a rope is wound around the runners, serving as a brake. With this precaution and careful handling a sled cannot get away from you.

HORSE HAULING LOADED SLED ON LAKE LINDEMANN

Apr. 7.

Warm weather again. We took our sleds up to the Summit in 3 $^1/_2$ hours loaded up 300 lbs. each and returned to Lindemann in 5 $^1/_2$ hrs. (a 20 mile trip). The grade from Summit down is a dangerous one and it is difficult to manage a sled here. Sometimes a sled handled carelessly came tearing down the grade and everybody shouted to clear the track. One warning was sufficient and sleds were yanked off to one side to give the runaway a clear path. In most cases such sleds would crash into a stack of provisions down below, scattering the goods in all directions, although the latter are bound fast with ropes.

OX HAULING
LOADED SLED OVER
LAKE LINDEMANN

A DOG TEAM ON
LAKE LINDEMANN

Apr. 8.

Having a severe attack of snow-blindness, I was compelled to rest and nurse my eyes. A visit to Dr. Frizell, who happened to be camped in the neighborhood, cost me $10.00. The remedy was boracic acid, dissolved in water to be applied as a wash, keeping the eyes well shaded—the least ray of light causes acute pain. (Imagine your eyes filled with grains of sand and the lids grinding against that—the agony of snow-blindness cannot be better illustrated.) This irritation makes one blink frequently and every time the lid closes you suffer intense pain. For 3 days and nights I remained inside the tent, unable to get a wink of sleep. I sat up nights resting my head in my hands, tears streaming from my eyes and cannot accurately describe what I suffered.

Apr. 9-10.

Geo. hauled 300 lbs. each day, while I rested.

Apr. 11.

My eyes are in much better condition but the weather is far too stormy to risk a trip to the Summit.

Apr. 12.

A little snow for a change—wet, and disagreeable weather. Each hauled a load of 300 lbs. and I wore a black mask to protect my eyes. (It is the white of the eye which becomes inflamed and the best protection is a mask with very small eye-holes.)

Apr. 13.

During the night we had a heavy fall of snow and the trail was completely covered up. We could not risk a trip today, for fear of getting caught in the mountain passes.

Apr. 14.

A party of men started out to break the trail and plodded through deep snow for 7 1/2 hours before they reached the Summit.

Apr. 15.

More snow and wet weather. We arose at 4 o'cl. and each hauled one load. For the next two days it snowed some more and we would not go out beyond the canyon. At

Lindemann the trail was in fine condition, so we conceived the idea of rigging up a mast on the sled and with a good breeze could easily take 2 sleds loaded up with 1,000 lbs., in one trip, as far as Lake Bennett. One man steered the sled with the gee-pole, while the other could sit on top of the load and rest. The wind was strong enough to carry the outfit along at a rapid pace, keeping the leader on the run. This was mere child's play as compared with the hard work we put in heretofore. The route to Lake Bennett was 6 ½ miles. (6 miles over Lake Lindemann and a ½ mile trail along Bell River, which connects both lakes.) Along the river the trail was in bad shape, worn down to the rocks and earth; this made sledding a difficult task. When we left Lindemann this morning it was very stormy, while at Bennett the weather was warm and pleasant. I neglected to wear my mask on several occasions, which again brought on a touch of snow-blindness. In the afternoon we carried 1200 lbs. on two sleds and the goods were cached on the ice of L. Bennett, near the town of Bennett. Here another batch of Canadian Police were stationed.

Apr. 19.

We both rested today.

Apr. 20.

I hauled the last load of 250 lbs. down from the summit while Geo. hauled several loads to Bennett. Again this morning it was freezing cold up in the passes, while in the after-

noon it was quite warm. (Sometimes, while tramping along in the passes, a snow storm would suddenly set in and then everybody made double quick time, so as to reach the canyon before the trail was covered up.) In 5 minutes time the weather changed from warm to freezing and one could easily lose his way in the blinding storm.

Next day we moved our camp outfit from L. Lindemann to a little patch of woodland, 3 miles below Bennett and on the opp. side of the lake. (Distance 9 ½ miles.) The tent was pitched on the beach, at the edge of the woods and good timber for boat-building was close at hand. (All the best timber was fast being used up for lumber.)

SAILING OUR SLED TO LAKE BENNETT OVER LAKE LINDEMANN. 1,200 POUNDS IN FIRST SLED.

A SIX-SPAN GOAT TEAM

OUR FIRST CAMP AT
LAKE BENNETT

BROOKLYN FRIENDS
AT LAKE BENNETT

OUR CAMP IN THE
WOODS AT LAKE
BENNETT

I AM HARD AT IT AT
LAKE BENNETT

Apr. 22.

Today we chopped down 5 big trees and marked them with name and date, for future use.

Apr. 23.

Hauled 350 lbs. each, from Bennett to our present camp and in the afternoon we dragged 4 of the logs down to our camp. These logs ranged from 12 to 20 ft. in length and from 5 to 10 in. in diameter.

Apr. 24.

Hauled 1000 lbs. this morning and 1200 lbs. in the afternoon, making use of the sail. This finished up all the sledding and packing, and we now intend to build our boat and later on go by the water route, all the way to Stewart River.

To give a clearer view of the vast amount of work thus far accomplished, I will here outline the route, showing the distances covered by sleds and packing. (37 ½ miles).

Apr. 25-26.

We had the first rain since passing the Summit. Enough logs were procured to erect a saw-pit, 7 ft. high, upon which the heavy logs must be rolled, for the purpose of sawing out the boards and ribs for the boat. The logs were rolled up on our skids, by means of a rope—then squared, and one inch boards marked out with chalk line, on both sides of the log. We used a 6 ft. saw—one man standing on the log above and the other on the ground, working the saw together.

It was no easy job for inexperienced hands to keep the saw straight on the line and if once you run off, it is difficult to work

SAWING LUMBER AT THE SAW PIT

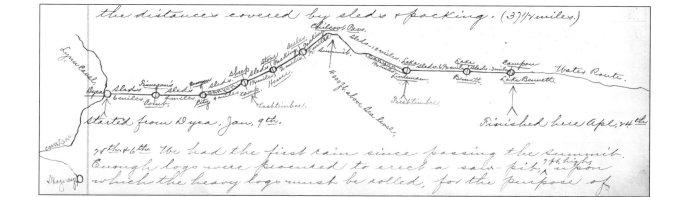

GEORGE AND I
SAWING OUT
LUMBER AT LAKE
BENNETT

the saw back again. My partner was a cabinet maker by trade and his knowledge of the handling of tools came in handy. Neither of us however, had any experience in boat-building; but we observed how others went at it and then got to work ourselves. A rough carpenter's bench was also erected alongside the saw-pit.

Apr. 27–May 3.

Started out for Dyea after mail and a supply of provisions (little odds and ends that were needed). The distance was 37 ½ miles. I left camp at 7:15 A.M. taking the sled with me. At the Lindemann P.O. I met the mail-carrier, who was also bound for Dyea. He was a jolly good fellow and pleasant company. We proceeded together up the canyon and then on to the Summit, chattering as we plodded along. It was very cold weather and a freezing head wind sweeping down from the Summit made it anything but a pleasant trip. The sled was left at Crater Lake. (My goods were to be hauled from Dyea to Canyon City then forwarded via the overhead cable to the Summit, from which point I could haul them back to camp on my sled.) After

crossing the Summit we encountered very mild weather. The trail from Stone House to Canyon City was [a] muddy one and the snow was fastly melting away. One could hardly believe Sheep Camp to be the same town we camped in not so long ago. Where the main trail formerly was, we found an open river and were forced to wade through some of its side channels, while others had a log thrown across, which served as a bridge.

On the level stretch of country, extending from Canyon City to Dyea, the snow had almost entirely disappeared. I arrived at Dyea 6:15 P.M. all tired out and very hungry (as usual).

At Field's store, our former home, I found our old friend, J.R. Dickinson from Sumner, Washington, who was with the Thorpe outfit last fall. Dickinson was making a little money selling potatoes, which he had forwarded to him from his father's farm in Sumner. I purchased my provisions, secured some mail and remained at Dyea until May 2d. My goods were forwarded to Sheep Camp and Dickinson also had some potatoes sent along, which he intended to sell at Bennett. (Charges were 4 ½ cts. a lb. to the Summit, 18 miles.) We stopped at Sheep Camp and next day went on to the Summit, but could not locate the goods until late in the afternoon; so we decided to stop over on the Pass for the night. A bunk-house was found, where the charges were 50 and 75 cts. respectively for bunk and meals. Spending a night on Chilcoot Pass was an experience neither of us had figured on—but I was glad of the opportunity. The bunk-house was an ordinary board affair with canvas roof and fitted up with board bunks. It was a case of furnishing your own blankets and going to bed with all your clothes on, unless you want to freeze to death. Luckily for us Dickinson had two pair of blankets. After partaking of a big dish of ham, beans and eggs, we spent the evening chatting with the police and at 9 o'clock turned into our bunks. It was mighty cold up here at this hour. (While the days may be warm, the nights are always cold.) Of course we had no fire in the shanty—wood costed 5 cts. per lb. delivered at the Summit. I had on wet socks, but dared not take them off, lest I freeze my feet. Sleep was entirely out of the question under the circumstances. We simply lay there, in the hard board bunk, shivering with cold and longing for morning and the cheering rays of the sun.

Several times during the night, I was forced to get up and stamp out my feet, to keep them from becoming entirely numb. It seemed an age until dawn. I rose early, got a nice warm breakfast and after moving around a little, felt quite comfortable again. I shall not so soon forget this night on Chilcoot Pass, but would not have missed it for anything.

May 4.

Hauled my 170 lbs. of provisions and Dickinson's 200 lbs. of potatoes, to Bennett. This was an awful trip. When I left Lindemann for Dyea, a week ago, the lake was covered with snow. Since then the snow had melted and in its place the ice

was covered with 6 inches of water. This meant 6 miles of wading in ice cold water, for along the shore there was slush 2 ft. deep, where one would sink to his knees at every step. My feet were soon numb from the cold and Dickinson suffered likewise. Once out on the lake, however, there was no chance for rest; so we kept at it and never stopped until we reached Bell River.

At this point there was no trace of snow left, so we had our goods hauled by wagon to Bennett. (charges $^{1}/_{2}$ cts. a lb.). At Bennett we stopped at Thorpe's Hotel, a comfortable log house, owned by the same Thorpe who tried to make the overland trail with the cattle last year.

The cattle were taken to Bennett and slaughtered and Thorpe opened up a hotel and restaurant, which paid pretty well. The floor was our bed and 50 cts. was charged for the privilege of stretching your weary body on solid boards—no blankets furnished, and meals costed $1.00.

May 5.

Dickinson sold his potatoes to the police at 10 cts. a lb. And in the afternoon we hauled my goods over Lake Bennett, down to the camp. Geo. had become very much alarmed over my long delay, thinking some harm had befallen me. Dickinson remained with us a few days and again returned to Dyea.

May 6.

Sawed our first 70 ft. of boards today, from the logs we had previously secured in the woods.

BUILDING OUR BOAT
AT LAKE BENNETT

CUTTING OUR OARS

May 7-11.

Sawed 40 ft. more. Next day was bad weather, so we rested. On the 9th and 10th we sawed 70 ft. each day and on the 11th 50 ft., besides some ribs for the boat.

May 12.

Commenced building our boat. All boards and ribs were planed off nicely. It was quite a difficult problem to make a well shaped boat, but ours turned out all right and looked as neat and trim as any of them.

May 19.

I puddled in water and mud all the way to Bennett and back to get our mail. The soft weather is melting the snow and the ice on Lake Bennett is honey-combed and very unsafe.

May 20.

Commenced cutting out 3 sets of oars, also several long sweep-oars. These were cut and shaped from small trees. Our boat was fitted up with a rudder, which came in handy sailing over the lakes—but in going down swift rivers, where quick action is essential, a long sweep-oar was the proper thing. The seams of our craft were plugged with oakum and pitched, to make them water-tight.

May 28.

During the night a severe storm broke up the ice in the lake and it is now floating away with the current. For several days past, boats were passing by here, along the narrow spaces of open water, in constant danger of being hemmed in by the ice.

May 29.

Our boat is now finished. It is a 22 ft. boat, flat bottom, with 6 in. keel, 5 $\frac{1}{2}$ ft. beam, pointed bow and square stern—fitted up with a mast, an 8 x 10 sail, 3 sets of oars, 2 sweep-oars, rudder and pump. The sail was made from canvas sacks, well sewed together, with loops for the guy ropes, so it could be shifted readily, according to the breeze.

May 30.

Before leaving here it was necessary to procure a miner's license and also have the boat registered by law. Further, a fee was exacted for the privilege of cutting the timber used for the boat. We got around that by producing a receipt for 250 ft. of lumber, supposedly purchased from a party named Hughes, who had a license for cutting timber and made a regular business of selling these fake receipts bearing his signature for $1.00 each. The free miner's license I obtained for $10.00. It granted me the privilege for one year, to mine, hunt and fish and cut timber, for my own use only. All boats when registered, were given a number—ours was #2,037. This enabled the authorities to keep a record of all boats and the occupants thereof, so in case of accidents or other complications, the police could readily identify the owners of every boat.

May 31.

During the night another storm raged hereabout and our boat was damaged some by pounding on the rocks. It was repaired at once and the outfit placed on board, preparatory to our departure for Stewart River on the following day.

The weather is pleasant and warm and in the woods numerous birds are chirping their merry tunes. There were two birds in particular, whose notes attracted my attention. The one could be heard regularly every day at 5 A.M. and again at 9 in the evening. Here is an exact reproduction of his merry tune.

He would keep that up for an hour at a time. The other one sang during the day in this fashion.

There was a certain bird called the Camp-robber that would sneak around the camp and eat anything in sight. The hawks devour these birds, whenever opportunity affords. Frequently we hear the pitiful cries of these camp-robbers, as they flit from tree to tree, with a hawk in close pursuit. Pretty soon their cries die out and we know that the hawk has again demonstrated his superior strength and ferocity and is perhaps at that moment tearing to pieces the more tender body of his fleeing victim. Even in this far-away wild country, where one grows accustomed to most anything, we stop to ponder over the murderous work of this hawk and express a desire to get a good shot at him; but he is too tricky a bird and keeps well out of range.

CAULKING OUR BOAT

GEORGE AND I READY FOR TRIP DOWN LAKES AND RIVERS, LAKE BENNETT, JUNE I, 1898

OUR BOAT SAILING ALONG

SIX CHICAGO BOYS LOADING A SCOW

June 1.

At last we are ready for the trip inland via the lakes and rivers. We arose at 3:30 adjusted our packages and sacks in the boat and left this dear old spot (the scene of our best efforts) at 10:30. It was a beautiful summer's day, with not the faintest trace of a breeze.

A hundred boats are within sight now, all bound for the Yukon River. Neither of us has had much experience in the handling of boats (my partner was absolutely green in this respect) and a new experience is in store for us—but again it is a case of do the best you can. We rowed until noon, when a brisk breeze sprang up. The sail was hoisted and in a jiffy our boat sped along over the water at a rapid pace.

What a pleasant recreation, in contrast to previous experience—but all is not smooth sailing, as future events will show. One man does the steering and the other manipulates the sail—it is great sport. Before we left this morning my attention was attracted to a thin curl of smoke, arising between the tree-tops near the camping ground. Geo. said it was nothing serious, so no further attention was paid to it. But after we had been under way one half hour, a great cloud of smoke was observed arising from the woods we had just left—pretty soon the entire woods were one roaring mass of flame, eating its way up the hill-side, to the mountain beyond. The pitch-covered spruce trees made good fuel for the flames and that woods was like a roaring furnace. Carelessness on Geo.'s part was the cause of this fire and a little water at the time would have prevented the spread of the flames.

He had emptied the ashes from our stove right near the camp, where there were lots of dry chips of wood strewn all over the ground and that is how the fire originated. A heavy punishment is meted out to anyone leaving a fire behind him when breaking camp and such gross carelessness is just what caused the tremendous forest fires all along the route. We were told later on that the police had come down from Bennett at the time, to investigate the matter. Luckily for us, the party camped near us in the woods, pretended not to know our names, nor boat number, thus saving both from punishment.

The hundreds of boats, with sails spread, all speeding in the same direction, were a fine sight to behold. Some of the boys would challenge us for a race and I must say our boat could hold its own. Cariboo Crossing was reached at 6 P.M. A river connects Bennett and Tagish lakes. The Crossing is at the head of the river. It is the point where herds of cariboo are in the habit of crossing the river, on their journey southward, before approach of Winter. The water is shallow and we had the misfortune to run aground on the sandy bottom. Then it was a case of get out and push until we reached deeper water, where the current carried us along nicely again. We have already learned that the deeper water is always in the swift current; right here it runs along the left bank of the river. While sailing over Lake Bennett, I had out a trolling line and caught a fine 2 $\frac{1}{2}$ lb. trout. At the head of Tagish Lake we pulled ashore near a nice patch of woodland and camped for the night. The fish was fried and both of us enjoyed a good hearty supper. Then we smoked our pipes and sat around telling stories.

It was too much trouble to pitch the tent, so we just spread out our sleeping bags and slept aboard the boat. This made a rather lofty berth and to guard against rolling into the water, two oars were stuck up on each side of the boat.

The nights are always very cool and sleeping-bags come in handy. Aside from affording protection against the cold winds (for they are made of heavy duck and lined with blankets), one can cover up completely, by pulling the hood down over the face and buttoning it up, thus shutting out the mosquitoes. The latter are a veritable pest and would eat you up, if given half a chance.

June 2.

Had breakfast at 5:30 and left here at 6:30 sailing down Tagish Lake. This was a stormy trip; the winds came sweeping down over the lake with great force, from the direction of Little and Big Windy Arm,* on the right (extensions of Tagish Lake). We were told that one always encounters rough weather on this lake. The 6 in. keel on our boat was of material assistance in holding the boat to the breeze—still, we drifted some. It was very difficult to manage a boat without a keel and several of these drifted on to the island in the middle of the lake and struck the rocks, where they were wrecked. Our boat shipped water at every pitch, as we sailed through the roughest part of it. For a time it was pretty serious business, the boat rolling and

*Little Windy Arm is today known as Windy Arm. Big Windy Arm is today known as Taku Arm.

THE KITCHEN ON BOARD OUR BOAT

POLICE AT TAGISH HOUSE INSPECTING BOATS COMING DOWN THE RIVER

WAITING FOR
CLEARANCE PAPERS
AT TAGISH HOUSE

ALONG THE FIFTY
MILE RIVER

THREE INDIAN PRISONERS AT
TAGISH HOUSE. HANGED AT
DAWSON CITY, NOVEMBER 1, 1898,
FOR COMMITTING MURDER

THE BANKS OF THE
FIFTY MILE RIVER

plunging in a frightful way. Every now and then the pump was brought into service. Geo. was steering for a time and in a careless moment allowed the boat to swing around with the rolling waves and we came very near being swamped. But the sail was lowered at once and after righting the boat we had no further trouble. Arrived at Tagish House (police headquarters) 3 P.M. Here all boats were called ashore to be inspected. Search was made for liquors or tobacco.

After inspection the O.K. slip had to be turned in at headquarters and then clearance papers were issued. We wanted to save time and did not have our boat inspected at all, but bribed one of the officers with a dollar bill and secured our inspection receipt at once. There were close on 300 men standing in line, waiting to reach headquarters. I held my position until evening, when all were given a number for a place in the line next day. My number was 281 and it was written on a little round gum wad, this probably being the most convenient material on hand.

June 3.

Held my position in line until 3 P.M. when I was enabled to reach headquarters and secure our papers. We left Tagish House at 4 P.M. The weather was rough but we made fine time and before evening were camped at the foot of Marsh Lake. The lower end of this lake is shallow water—also the river connecting Tagish and Marsh lakes. We ran aground at both these places, but had no difficulty in clearing the boat.

June 4.

After Marsh Lake came Fifty Mile River, which had a moderate current. Here we could rest ourselves and enjoy a smoke allowing the boat to float along with the current. The banks of this river were lined

ENTRANCE TO MILES' CANYON

with vegetation, which was already well advanced in growth. Several parties had warned us to pull ashore, before we reach Miles' Canyon and walk along the high bank to observe how other boats were piloted through.

The river narrows down suddenly and the current is very swift. A little further on comes the canyon (a dangerous bit of water) and 2 miles below that the celebrated White

SHOOTING THROUGH MILES' CANYON

Horse Rapids we had heard so much about. We were just a little tardy in heeding the warning and before either one was aware of it, the swifter current had already caught the boat and it was a physical impossibility to

ALONG MILES'
CANYON

ALONG MILES'
CANYON

reach the shore. But I jumped forward into the bow of the boat and threw the line to some fellow on shore—but he could not hold the swiftly moving boat and was almost dragged out into the river over one of the other boats tied up there. In less time than it takes to tell, our boat swung around, stern forward, as we sped along with the ever-increasing current. We were now in the narrow river, which rushes along madly on its winding course between the mountains and leads to the canyon, which is a narrow opening between high bluffs. For a moment we were dumbfounded at the thought of traversing these strange and dangerous waters without any knowledge whatever of the proper course to take. But there was no time for reflection—a few seconds hesitation may mean the loss of the outfit, to say nothing of our lives. In my imagination I could fancy the boat rolling and pitching in the mad waters and all of a sudden plunging over the Rapids. The rope was already gathered in and in three jumps I reached the sweep-oar in the stern of the boat. Geo. remained at the oars and I shouted to him, "We are in for it—lets try to keep cool and do the best we can!" (But the hardest part of it was to keep cool.) All this transpired in a few seconds. In spite of all the danger and excitement I could not help laughing when I saw Geo. gazing at me with pale countenance and dumb as an oyster. Already we could hear the roaring of the waters in the Canyon, some distance ahead. I was badly frightened myself, but for some unknown reason could not control my feelings and fairly shook with laughter. In spite of the danger there was something very fascinating to this hair-raising experience. With several hard swift pulls the boat was righted and we sped on at a lively clip. The sharp turns of the river keep one guessing, because you cannot look ahead for any distance and never know what to expect around the next bend. All of a sudden the river widens out a bit and just beyond is the narrow entrance to the canyon; the roaring of the waters becomes deafening. Just off to the right we spied several boats tied up at the shore—but it is already too late to pull over there. Had we taken a look at the course, as originally intended, we would feel more confident of a safe trip—under the circumstances however, it was pretty risky business. My eyes were glued to the narrow opening in the rocks ahead and I steered straight for it, at the same time directing Geo. how to row. Something is surely going to happen—I feel it coming. Into the narrow passage our boat shot, like a flash. On either side were jagged rocks—we must keep in the middle, right in the worst of it. How that water did tumble and foam and roar! There are 2 of these narrow shoots here, a wider bit of water connecting them. It is very difficult to keep the boat on a straight course. All of a sudden it made a lurch and swung around so fast, I could not prevent it. With a mighty tug at the oar I attempted to swing it into position, when, to our horror, the oar snapped in two. Glancing up at the top of the bluff, I could see a number of men, with anxious faces, watching the outcome of our perilous situation. Before I could begin to place the spare oar in position, the boat had swung completely around, stern forward. (Had we not taken the precaution of carrying this extra sweep-oar, I might never have lived to write up the story of this trip). Already we'd reached the wider channel—the spare oar was in its place and the boat rightened once more. It was a narrow escape—shooting out of the first narrow cut, the rocks were missed by less than five feet! Not a word was uttered at the critical moment—I held my breath, prepared for the worst and think Geo. did the same. Into the second narrow cut we plunged, the boat pitching in the mad waters. All this is a great deal more than we bargained for—I was wishing we were on shore. As the boat shot out of the Canyon into the wider river, some boats were seen on the right bank. The dreaded White Horse Rapids are coming next—but

we had enough sport for one day and made a desperate effort to reach shore. A raft, stranded on the rocks, is just ahead—we will surely plunge right into it. The current is swift and the river bottom full of rocks. We are carried down stream some distance in our attempt to cross the current. But luck is with us again—the boat just misses the wreck and we are approaching the shore. Suddenly we hit a rock!—another one, and yet another. The boat comes to a sudden stop and we are stuck fast, 20 feet from the shore. A line is hastily cast and held by half a dozen willing hands—we are safe now. The water is not very deep, so we pull on our rubber boots, get into the water and try to push the boat off the rocks—but in vain! The swift current almost carries my feet from under me. Our boat was made fast

ALONG MILES' CANYON

THE OUTLET OF MILES' CANYON

RAFT STRANDED ON ROCKS JUST BELOW MILES' CANYON

with the line. Once again we are on land—how solid the earth feels under my feet! We could not clear the boat until our whole outfit had been carried ashore and then it was found that it had sprung a leak.

June 5.

Spent the greater part of the day in overhauling the boat. Our experience in the canyon had given us a little scare, so a pilot was hired to take us through the Rapids. His services cost $25.00—but he would not consent to take the full load through, on account of the boat drawing too much water and [in] addition to this the 6 in. keel made it a dangerous venture among the rocks. Before starting out, however, we walked down to the Rapids and watched the boats and scows coming through. Some got along very well—others hit the rocks and had a hole punched in the bottom. Before the occupants had a chance to reach shore, just below the Rapids, these boats were filled with water and the sacks of provisions were floating out into the river. These poor unfortunates were to be pitied. After all the hard labor and hardship endured to get along this far and then to see the boats and outfits lost or destroyed in a few moments, is indeed a hard blow. I wondered how our boat would come through. After leaving the Canyon there is a series of minor rapids, then comes a wide canyon, with swift water and at the end of this, the White Horse Rapids, where the river narrows down to about 30 ft., with a sudden drop of 6 feet. On either side are low, flat rocks, and extreme care must be taken in coming through; otherwise one is apt to land on the rocks and that means the wrecking of the boat.

SHOOTING THE WHITE HORSE RAPIDS

June 6.

Our pilot came along today, to take us through the rapids. At the first attempt to swing out into the deeper channel, we again hit the rocks near the shore and stuck fast, but the boat was not damaged. All hands got out into the water and pulled the boat up stream about 100 ft. The second attempt was successful and we soon reached deep water, speeding along at a lively pace. The pilot did the steering, with the sweep oar, while Geo. and I held the oars, ready to pull as the pilot directed. Onward we sped, the boat bobbing up and down in the rough waters and the spray constantly dashing over us. Just before we arrived at the canyon, this side of the White Horse, the pilot insisted that we land and unload some of the outfit, since the boat was drawing too much water. He was afraid we might hit the rocks in the canyon and we quickly decided to land. After unloading something like 1200 lbs. we turned into the canyon, where the current is very swift. Faster and faster the boat plunged along, until the White Horse is reached. We are going so fast, it takes our breath away. Finally we shoot through the narrow White Horse and suddenly plunge down the fall of 6 ft. out into the wider channel and the danger is over. The current is not near so swift here and we found a good landing place about ¼ mile below the Rapids. In the afternoon our 1200 lbs. of provisions were packed down to the boat and then it was time for a rest. My partner Geo. was very disagreeable at times—he continually worried over the outcome of the trip. I let him have his way in everything, just so as not to get into any arguments. He even threatened me, but I realized that the worry and excitement had a bad effect on him and asked him to be reasonable. (I realized later on that it was a great mistake to let him have his way in everything and found it necessary to take effective measures to bring him to his senses.)

June 7.

It was 7 P.M. before we continued our long inland trip down Fifty Mile River. Nothing of interest was observed along here and we camped near Lake Le Barge. While the current is not swift, the river is full of sand bars—we ran aground on these twice. (The setting sun at 9 P.M. was a beautiful sight to behold and one I shall not so soon forget.)

SHOOTING THE WHITE HORSE RAPIDS

June 8.

Had an early breakfast and started down the lake. The water at the head of Le Barge is shallow and also full of sand bars. Here again our boat stuck fast, but it was only a temporary delay. A fine breeze sprang up, the sail was hoisted and we had a chance to rest, until 11 o'clock, when a perfect calm set in. Then we rowed on slowly and by 12 o'cl. reached a large island, in the middle of the lake, where lunch was prepared. It is mountainous country all along here. At Le

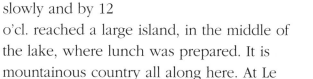

SHOOTING THE WHITE HORSE RAPIDS

Barge the mountains are devoid of vegetation. (These are called "Bald Knobs.") We put in a hard days' work today—6 hours of rowing in a blazing sun is no pleasure. Half past 6 found us camped at the foot of the big island. At 9 P.M. it is still light enough to read a newspaper in the open air, while in mid-summer there is no night at all—only semi-darkness for a few hours.

June 9.

A strong headwind was encountered and we rowed but 10 miles this day and camped in the woods, near the foot of Le Barge.

June 10.

One half hours' rowing brought us to Thirty Mile River, a swift bit of water. It is the head of Lewis River and for 30 miles one is constantly in danger, on account of the rocks and innumerable gravel bars. Here is where the flat bottom boat comes in handy—in fact it is the only practical one on waters like Thirty Mile, on account of the rocks. We got down this river 10 miles today and decided to rest, in order to gain our equilibrium. Speeding down a river at a 12 mile [an hour] clip, constantly dodging rocks and gravel bars, makes one's hair stand on end. Besides, it is a winding course and one never knows what to expect around the next bend. Here and there one sees the wreck of a boat loom up ahead, smashed against some rock and generally standing up on end, as a warning to others. The occupants of these boats were lucky indeed, if they

managed to save their lives. We were speeding down the left bank at a lively pace (Geo. at the oars, ready to pull at a second's notice and I manipulating the sweep-oar). Coming around a sharp bend in the river, I observed a sign, some distance away, stuck up near the water, with red lettering on it.

We felt instinctively that it was a danger signal, although it could not be read from that distance. Our eyes were riveted on that sign for the next few moments, until we got close enough to read these terrorizing words: "Danger—keep to the right!" At the same time we observed the rocks, right in our path and the wreck of a boat, sticking up over the water. There was no need of giving any orders here. Each one realized that his life depended on the next move and knew just what to do. But I did shout to George: "Pull for your life!" And he did pull for all he was worth. It is no easy matter to pull across stream in such swift current and distances are deceiving, because the boat travels so fast. The way Geo. tugged at those oars, raising up out of his seat and I working that sweep-oar in double quick time, was a lesson for an expert. But again we were rewarded for our efforts and cleared those rocks by 3 or 4 feet, shooting on down the right bank. This was one of the closest calls we had at any time, but when it was all over we could not help laughing over it. Once we plunged right over a flat rock, without sustaining the least damage. Another time I made a serious mistake. Instead of holding the boat to the left bank, where the deep channel was, I steered down mid-stream. The boat hit one rock and we wondered what would happen next. Again it struck—and then four or five times more in rapid succession, suddenly coming to a dead stop. There we were stuck fast on the flat rocks, in the middle of this narrow river. Several boats darted by us, to the left. The occupants barely had time to glance our way, for they had their own hands full. As luck would have it, the boat did not swing, but remained in position with the current. Had it swung around, nothing could have saved us from being swamped, as the pressure of the current was strong enough to upset the boat. I dared not take my hands off the sweep-oar, so George got out and tried to push the boat off the rocks. After 10 minutes hard work he succeeded and quickly jumped aboard. We managed to steer off into deeper water and all was lovely once more. The keel probably saved us from having a hole punched in the bottom—but without it, perhaps the boat would not have hit the rocks at all. This Thirty Mile River is the worst bit of water along the whole route. Speeding along at the rate of 12 or 15 miles an hour, we could see the big rocks in the clear water, never knowing at what instant the boat might strike. It kept our hair standing on end the entire distance, and yet there is a certain charm to the situation, which almost makes one wish for more excitement. Somewhere along here we saw the first bunch of Indians since leaving Sheep Camp. Several of them standing near the water's edge with hair disheveled, shouting at us as we passed by. I tried to snap the camera on them, but the attempt was a failure; we were moving too fast.

June 11.

Arose at 5:30 and after a hurried breakfast, left here 7:30. It rained a little last night, so we had our tent up. Some of the boys managed to catch a few nice fish in one of the creeks near here and we shared in the feast. At 11 o'cl. we arrived at the Hootalingua River, where another batch of Canadian Police inspected our papers. There is some flat country along here and the shores are lined with woods and thick brush. We have passed the most dangerous points now, but the Five Finger and Rink rapids are yet to come. Two o'cl. found us under way again and we did not camp until 7:30. It was a very warm day—and only last night it was freezing cold. But that is one of the good features of the Alaskan summers—while the days may be warm, the nights are always cold.

June 12.

Started out for a 50 mile run down Lewis River. This is but a moderate current, and the water is very muddy. A few gravel bars and islands are scattered here and there. At 8:30 we passed the Big Salmon River where the numbers of all boats were recorded as they came by. The Little Salmon River was passed at 4 P.M.

CANADIAN POLICE HEADQUARTERS AT BIG SALMON RIVER, WHERE NUMBERS OF ALL BOATS ARE RECORDED AS THEY PASS BY

LOADED SCOW
WITH HORSE ON THE
LEWIS RIVER

PREPARING LUNCH
ALONG THE LEWIS
RIVER

Gold was supposed to have been found along both these rivers. The Lewis R. widens out here and this is a pleasure jaunt, as compared with the swift and treacherous Thirty Mile River. All we had to look out for was to keep in the main channel, where the water was very deep and we simply floated with the current. The vast lowlands on either side of the river, with high mountains in the distance are coming into view. Whenever we spied an island or a bar ahead, we pulled away from it in time and then let the current carry us along. Once the distance was miscalculated and our boat drifted right on to the corner of an island, one current catching the bow and the other the stern. It was a gravel bottom and the pressure of the two currents forced the boat aground harder every moment. Both of us worked hard to free the boat, but we could not make the main channel and were compelled to float around the island. Luckily for us it was a clear channel and at the lower end of the island it carried us right into the proper course. It was 8 P.M. when good camping ground was found and that ended this day's travel. There is plenty of dry wood all along here, but we always like to camp either in the woods or on some bar. The first thing we do is to build a big fire and drive the mosquitoes away, otherwise we have absolutely no chance of rest. Even with fire and smoke in front of and all around us, these hungry "skeeters" will get at you.

June 13.

Today we started out at 6:30 proceeding down Lewis R. until 12:30 when hunger drove us to shore. We are always hungry and glad when the hour for our next meal is at hand. One hour later we are again en route and at 4 P.M. landed near Five Finger Rapids. We wished to take a look at the course, before venturing through. A mile tramp through the woods brought us to the Rapids and from one of the high bluffs along shore we could observe how the boats were steered through. At this point there are five high rocks, projecting out of the water. To the left of these is a wide channel, which is full of rocks and not navigable. The proper course is along the right bank and runs between the fifth rock and the high bluff on the shore; a very narrow passage. It is not a dangerous undertaking,

but care must be exercised in coming through this narrow space, for the cross-current which comes tearing around the rock is apt to swing the boat and the latter may be swamped, if handled carelessly. There were great forest fires all along here and the ashes lay 3 or 4 in. deep; the dust almost choked us. Returning to our boat, we at once started out and passed the Rapids at 5:30. Here again the current is very swift and when the narrow cut is reached, the boat fairly plunges along. The very thing we were so anxious to prevent, did happen. Geo. was steering and allowed the boat to swing, when we hit the cross-current, in spite of my warning, "Don't let her swing." Nothing serious occurred however, only it gave us a lively shaking up. The boat rolled and pitched in the rushing waters and a few minutes later we were again safe in smoother water, but the current was still a swift one. Geo. was rather touchy and felt hurt at my remark, while I had no intention of offending him—it was simply a warning. He became impertinent, abusive and there was some talk of parting at the next landing place. He had his own way too much and could not bear the slightest interference in anything, without becoming ruffled. We camped at 6:30 and came to a thorough understanding, so as to avoid any complications in the future. (I state these disagreeable matters so plainly, simply to show what caused them and further to make the point clear, that the very best of friends can get into arguments when they are compelled to be in each other's company constantly; especially when on a trip of this kind. I have

seen so many fights between former companions up in this country, that I wondered if the food or the climate had anything to do with their ill tempers.) From this time on the good feeling that had existed between us had slackened somewhat, as later developments will show. Each performed exactly the same work—one day I did the cooking, next day was his turn; so also with the rowing or steering of the boat, sawing up firewood—in short, everything. This was one way of preventing any arguments from that direction. The policy to be adhered to is "give and take," but when one of the parties is stubborn, then there is trouble in store for both. To part and join a stranger may be like going from the frying-pan into the fire.

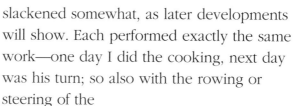

FIVE FINGER RAPIDS. THE PROPER COURSE IS THROUGH THE OPENING AT RIGHT.

ROUGH WATER IN FIVE FINGER RAPIDS

FORT SELKIRK ON THE YUKON RIVER

INDIAN LOG HOUSES AT FORT SELKIRK ON THE YUKON RIVER

June 14.

Having enjoyed a good night's rest and hearty breakfast the trip was again continued at 8 o'cl. Half an hour later we passed the Rink Rapids, which are not at all dangerous, if you keep to the right bank. The current is swift and the boat takes a plunge once in a while, but as compared with the White Horse it is mere child's play. We arrived at Fort Selkirk on the Yukon River, at 8 P.M. The fort lies on the left bank, immediately below the junction of Lewis and Pelly rivers, which form the Yukon. The N.W. Mounted Police are stationed here and a band of Indians live at the further end of the settlement. The evening was spent with the Indians and the police. The boat can always be left tied up anywhere along the bank and strange to say, we never missed a single thing. No one would think of entering the boat without permission. And yet, what an easy matter it would be for anyone to steal away with the boat and outfit.

June 15.

At last we get a good look at the Yukon that great river, over 2000 miles in length,* and at this point about ³/₄ of a mile wide. We left the fort at 7:45. High bluffs line the shore on the left and to the right we see a solid mass of burnt rock, black in color. It was such an unusual sight, that we investigated and found the rock had a ring to it, like metal. It runs up to a heighth of 50 ft. It is 1 mile in length; semi-circular in formation. In years gone by, this curious rock may have been the crater of some giant volcano. Further on are the mountains, on both sides of the river; the scenery is fine. Islands, sand and gravel bars are numerous. The current is moderate and the water muddy, similar to Lewis River. We put in a long day and camped on the bank of the Yukon at 8 P.M.

June 16.

Again we started out at 7:45. Aside from the fine scenery, there is nothing of interest along here. White River (a tributary of the Yukon, so named on account of the milky color of the water) was passed at 6:30 P.M. Snow and ice was seen along the banks here and this is the middle of June. In the afternoon it rained a little for a change and 7 o'cl. again found us in camp.

---

*The Yukon is actually 1,979 miles long.

June 17.

Seven o'cl. and we are off once more, reaching Stewart River at 9 o'clock. We are now about 530 miles from Dyea. There is an island directly opposite the mouth of this river and in order to land on the Stewart, one must hold the boat to the right bank. We landed on the second island below the mouth, where several hundred tents were pitched. While floating down the right bank, I noticed some fallen trees hanging out over the water and called Geo.'s attention to them. He thought there was plenty of time for steering away from them and waited until it was too late. As a result, the mast crashed into the tree and broke off at the base, ripping up the seat upon which I was sitting at the time, handling the oars. But I cleared out just an instant before the crash, thus escaping serious injury. (Masts should really be lowered after leaving Lake Le Barge, for the river currents carry a boat along fast enough, without the use of a sail.) The greater part of our outfit will be left on the island (cached), and the rest of it will be taken up the Stewart River, when we start out on our prospecting trip. The cache in the woods was made by sawing off 3 of the smaller trees, about 20 ft. above ground— then we nailed on some cross-pieces and placed the goods on this platform, so they would be out of reach of the animals. A piece of heavy canvas or a tarpaulin is then tied over all so as to keep out the rain. Waited for a party of two, who were coming down the river on a scow and promised to meet us here, but we saw no trace of them.

The large boat could not be used in the trip up Stewart River (against the current) so we will have to build a smaller boat. Some pushed their boats up stream with long poles, but our plan is to walk along the bank and pull the boat on a long line.

ALONG THE YUKON RIVER

June 22.

Commenced sawing out lumber for the smaller boat— but there was no dry timber and wet logs are a tough proposition, so this work was abandoned. Then we tried to narrow down the large boat to one— half its original dimensions and make that do; but it was such a wabbly affair we dared not make use of it.

AN ISLAND IN THE YUKON RIVER

OUR OUTFIT CACHED AT THE MOUTH OF STEWART RIVER ON AN ISLAND

MOUNTAINS ALONG THE STEWART RIVER

June 28.

Two Englishmen (Geo. Money from London and Bob Cheatham from San Francisco) happened along and offered us the use of their boat, in case we wished to join them. Reports from up the river were anything but encouraging, but we shall see for ourselves. Three months supply of provisions were placed in the boat and at 2 P.M. we started up the Stewart, 3 men pulling the boat along on the line, while the 4th steered, so as to keep it well out from shore. It was necessary to bridle the boat—this is done by running a slack rope from the bow to about ⅓ the length of the boat and the long rope is fastened to the middle of this loop, thus. (If the rope were fastened on the bow only, it would be impossible to keep the boat pointing off shore,

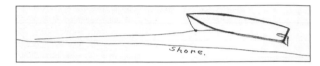

as in the illustration.) The idea of having the boat pointing off shore is for the purpose of avoiding the rocks, driftwood etc., along the water. Taking the rope over your shoulder and pulling against the current is very hard work. The banks are lined with thick brush, rocks and fallen trees—the latter being found where the bank caved in. Great stacks of driftwood are found, 20 ft. high in some places. We climbed over the top of these, passing the rope along from one to another and at the same time holding the boat in the current. In the beginning of summer, when the snow melts and increases the volume of water, the current is swift—at this season of the year it runs from 4 to 5 miles an hour. The river is full of sand and gravel bars. At times it was necessary to wade out into the river and push the boat over a bar—at such points we found a drop of from 1 to 2 ft. over the bar and it was all we could do to hold our boat, the pressure of the current being enormous. Then again, further travel along the bank was suddenly obstructed by high bluffs, which run up straight from the water. If these bluffs were not too high and our rope reached, we climbed over the top of them. Otherwise we were compelled [to] get into the boat and row across current, to the opposite bank. On such occasions considerable ground was lost, for the river is wide and in rowing across, the current carried us down stream—sometimes ¼ mile. In the evening we camped on an island and shot some squirrels, ducks and muskrats.

The mosquitoes almost ate us up alive—there are millions of them. Every day we waded in ice cold water, sometimes up to our waists and at night the wet clothes were dried at the campfire. The bed was prepared on the sand or gravel along shore—in the woods, or wherever a good spot was found to camp.

Timber is plentiful all along Stewart River. At night we are compelled to cover up with blankets completely, leaving only a small opening to breathe through. If this precaution were not taken, there would be no chance for rest, for the pesky mosquitoes are after you continually. The extreme cool nights are very refreshing however, and I always enjoyed a good night's rest.

June 29.

Met a party of St. Louis boys who were washing out flake gold with a rocker on one of the gravel bars. They obtained from 4 to $5.00 worth of flake gold per day each. We have been prospecting along all the gravel and sand bars, on the bluffs along the river and back into the woods, away from the water. This flake-gold is found every-where—but nowhere in paying quantity. A few days ago the St. Louis boys were up on a high bluff, across the river and there discovered a black bear with her cub. The old bear was frightened and scampered off through the woods, while the cub shinnied up a tree. One of the party climbed up after it, but the little one was game and fought him off. Then the tree was cut down again baby bear was equal to the occasion, for it

landed on all fours and quickly disappeared into the thick brush, where further pursuit would be in vain. When we heard this little bear story it whetted our appetite for game. Money, one of the St. Louis parties and myself took our Winchesters, crossed the river in a boat and climbed the high bluff in search of the bear. Not one of us ever had any experience in hunting bear, but we were looking for excitement of some kind. It was already late in the afternoon and we hunted around for 3 hours, with no result. A little later on however, we found the lair of bruin beside a big tree and the snug berth of the cub in some bushes nearby, but no trace of either mother or cub. The old one evidently had been scared away and did not return to her lair. We con-

AN ISLAND IN THE STEWART RIVER

ST. LOUIS BOYS AT WORK WITH A ROCKER ON THE STEWART RIVER

"LET'S WASH OUT A PANFULL OF THIS AND SEE WHAT THERE'S IN IT"

tented ourselves by admiring the beautiful scenery from the edge of the bluff and took the risk of being disabled by clouds of mosquitoes. No opportunity was lost in prospecting the ravines and creeks which empty into Stewart. The result was always the same; nothing but flake gold. Bad reports are heard, all along the line—but we have gone this far and will certainly continue the trip. Often we must tramp over heaps of broken rocks, along the shore where stones and earth slid down the mountain sides to the water's edge—our rubber boots are fast wearing out. It rained every day and in the afternoon, regular as the clock, we had a thunder storm. There are thousands of squirrels in the woods about here and the small lakes are fairly alive with ducks. Wild flowers are abundant and especially the wild rose—there are acres of them. Being fond of flowers, this was one of the pleasant surprises I met with in this far-away northern country—wild roses in such numbers were never thought of.

July 4.

It rained all day. Having no ammunition with which to celebrate the day, we decided to take a rest. In the afternoon Money and myself went out on a hunt for ducks, but succeeded in bagging only three. Moose tracks were discovered all over the flat, swampy regions and yet we were never rewarded with even a glimpse of one. The big game cannot be found along the river, but further back into the country there is plenty of it. We could not spare the time to go out on more extensive hunting expeditions. My partner's actions are becoming unbearable and there is every indication of a parting when we reach McQuestion River. (A tributary of the Stewart R. 110 miles up from its mouth.)

July 6.

We put in a very hard day's work—pulling our boat against unusually swift currents, and wading in water up to our waists half the time. In many places the high banks were undermined by the water. We walked over these dangerous spots, never knowing when they might cave in and land us in the river. Great chunks of earth were continually breaking loose and tumbling down into the water. Strange to say, we passed over all of the dangerous spots in safety. In the afternoon we discovered some blankets, clothing and packages of provisions, floating down the river. Evidently some one's boat had upset and the contents were carried away with the current. We just managed to fish up a large can of coffee and carried it along, to give to the unfortunate party, should we discover them. A little further on the bank projected out into the river, to a sharp point.

There was a swift current running off from the point and we had to apply our combined strength in pulling the boat around. Here is where the boat had upset and we found a party of three standing at the water's edge, wringing out their wet clothes. Most of their provisions and clothing were lost in the river and they were mighty glad to get back the coffee. They were fortunate enough to recover the boat, so they were not in such a bad plight after all. It was our turn next. Further on, while turning a sharp bend in the river, a stiff current was encountered and we could not pull the boat around. In fact we were barely able to hold it, until Money, who was steering, stood up in the bow and assisted us, by means of a long pole, which he rested on the river bottom and then threw his weight against like in an effort to push the boat along. The other three of us had the long rope over our shoulders, leaning forward and pulling with all our might. But the strain was too much and all of a sudden, the rope broke. The quick release from this strain caused us to pitch forward head first and we landed all in a heap. Glancing around hastily, we saw to our horror how Money was hurled headlong into the river. In a moment the boat swung around with the current and floated down stream. Money in the water, fighting for his life and our three months of provisions possibly lost, was anything but a pleasant situation. The under current pulled him down twice and no wonder for the poor fellow had on his rubber boots which filled with water and must have felt like lumps of lead on his feet. For a few moments we watched

for Money, in utter silence. Then, as he reappeared on the surface, all three shouted to him to swim after the boat. But the brave fellow needed no urging and knew just exactly what to do. With a mighty effort he struck out boldly for the boat and it was seen that the current carried him along much faster than it did the boat. So we ran down the bank, helter-skelter, through brush and over fallen trees, at the same time shouting words of encouragement to our brave companion. He kept at his task with a good will and swam $1/4$ mile down stream, before he caught up with the boat. His attempt to pull himself aboard over the side was a failure—but he was not discouraged and simply let go his hold and managed to get a grip on the rudder, where after several further attempts, he finally managed to climb aboard. A mighty shout arose from three throats as he did so. After resting for a few moments, to regain his wind, he calmly picked up the oars and rowed to shore where we were on hand to receive and congratulate him on his narrow escape. Everybody was very much excited at first, but now that Money and the boat were safe, we all had a good laugh over it, Money joining in, as heartily as the rest. Then we

OVERHANGING BANKS ALONG THE STEWART RIVER. GREAT CHUNKS OF EARTH WERE CONTINUOUSLY BREAKING LOOSE.

rowed across the river to a good camping ground and rested for the day, giving Money a chance to dry his clothes. Had our boat gone adrift there would be no supper for us, unless we could have managed to catch a fish. Not only that, but we would have been compelled to wait here until some boat came along to take us down the river.

July 7-8.

Passed Independence and Clear (or Clearwater) creeks, where we found a number of camps, and heard the same hard luck story—no gold discovered.

July 9.

My partner Geo. is worried and heartbroken over the failure of the trip, thus far. For some time past, in fact since our first rupture, I noticed that he sought in various ways to annoy me by his silly actions. When the same thing occurred again this noon, at lunch, it made me angry and I called him to account for it. He became enraged and swore, finally calling me by a vile name. Losing all control of myself, I jumped to my feet (he likewise) and asked him to stand up and fight.

It was the only thing I could do, for everything must come to an end some time. I need not minutely describe what happened—suffice it to say that he will never forget the severe drubbing I gave him. Even then he threatened to throw a big rock at me and only after repeated warning that he would get a worse dose of the same medi-

cine did he desist from his cowardly purpose. It was understood that when we reach the McQuestion River, our outfit would be divided equally and each could join whatever party he pleased. The balance of our goods, left at the island, were to be divided up later, at some time to be agreed upon, when both could be present. But the end was not yet. The journey up stream was continued until noon when we stopped to prepare lunch. I had just finished my meal and turned around to walk over the camp-fire, for the purpose of arranging some of the clothes I had hung to dry. To my surprise I saw Geo. standing about 10 paces away, with the Winchester rifle leveled at me, threatening to shoot if I approached him. It was such an unexpected turn of affairs, that for a few moments I was dumbfounded and speechless. After regaining my composure I asked him what he meant by this. (Even then I pitied him, for I knew that he was worried half to death and still smarting under the severe beating I gave him.) He acted like a crazy man and insisted on a fair division of the outfit, whereupon he was informed that the agreement entered into would be carried out to the letter, so far as I was concerned and that I would also take good care that he lived up to it. For just a moment I felt sorry that my gun was not handy, for he had me at a terrible disadvantage; but realizing that he was laboring under intense excitement, I simply insisted that he place the rifle back into the boat. This he bluntly refused to do, keeping his finger on the trigger and I really believe he would have shot me had I approached him. Again my anger got the best of me and I dared him to blaze away. His action so thoroughly enraged and disgusted me, that I carelessly took a chance, at the same time telling him that my only wish was his wife could see him standing there, pointing a gun at me. This seemed to have no effect on him however. At this stage of the dispute our mutual friend Money interfered and finally induced Geo. to put back the rifle. That ended the whole affair. (I did not intend, originally, to make any mention of this disgraceful incident, nor the previous one, but it would not be a full and accurate account of the trip, without them. It simply goes to show what may happen.) After this, few words passed between us—and then only when it could not be avoided. I was not thirsty for revenge, although there was ample cause for it.

July 12.

Arrived at the McQ. River at 2 P.M. and camped on the high bank to the left. (We were now 110 miles up the Stewart.) There were a number of tents pitched here and just above the mouth of the river was an Indian village.

The first thing on our minds was the dividing up of the outfit, as per agreement. This was no easy matter, as we soon discovered. Money and Cheatham were to divide it up—we to abide by their decision. With the provisions there was no trouble—but when it came to the tools and other implements, they knew not what to do. Surely they could not give one man a plane and the other an ax, or vice versa. So the judges decided they

could not divide it equally and do justice to both. Finally Money took me to one side and asked me to reconsider the matter, while Cheatham argued with Geo. The result of it all was that we did not part—I was willing to forgive Geo. yet I could never forget. It was arranged that the whole party continue on up McQ. River. This river is narrow, has a swift current and rapids, also sandbars. A good many people started out for Nelson Creek, 120 miles up the McQ. Some claimed that a little gold was found there, but the report was discredited.

MOUTH OF THE MCQUESTION RIVER

AN INDIAN COUPLE ON THE MCQUESTION RIVER

July 13.

The boat was trimmed down some to lighten it and part of the provisions cached in the woods. In the afternoon all hands

INDIANS AT THE
MCQUESTION RIVER

AN OLD, CRIPPLED
INDIAN,
MCQUESTION RIVER

INDIAN GIRL WITH
ROLL OF BIRCH BARK,
MCQUESTION RIVER

INDIAN FISH TRAP
MADE OF WILLOW
ON THE
MCQUESTION RIVER

paid the Indians a visit and had a good time. They are a dirty lot—worse than the Coast Indians, but more friendly. The Coast Indians come in contact with the Whites a great deal and have learned some of the tricks and ways of the world, but these fellows are quite ignorant and harmless. The hovels they live in have brush piled up on the outside, forming the walls and a bit of canvas stretched over this forms the roof. The squaws were busily engaged with the tanning of moose hides, or making up moccasins and other fancy articles. The men attend to the fishing and hunting. Those of the old bucks, that had a pipe, sat around smoking. One old fellow (a cripple) whose picture I had taken, begged for a bit of tobacco and seemed tickled to death when he got it. They live on salmon principally and have their willow fish-traps planted right near here, in the swift water. The trap is a long round basket, made from strips of willow and tapers to a small opening at one end. The fish, swimming up stream, float into this basket and cannot get out again. Besides salmon, they also find trout and pike in some of the streams and squirrels and small birds are on the bill of fare, now and then. In the line of big game there is moose, cariboo and black bear. Vegetation is now well advanced [and] wild roses and other pretty flowers cover the hillside.

July 14.

Started up the McQ. with our boat, at 9:30 this morning. As we passed the village, a bunch of Indian girls were taking a bath in the river. I tried to get a snapshot at them, but was a little too late—for when they discovered that something unusual was going on, they all made a break for shore. One little one, whose picture was secured, yelled murder when the Kodak was pointed at her. (Perhaps she was afraid the thing might go off.) We met many parties coming down the river and all of them make the same report, "nothing found." The bars were prospected thoroughly; but the further we advanced, the less colors were found. Every one coming down advised us not to go any further—so after tramping up stream 40 miles and finding still less colors, the trip was abandoned. A peculiar thing about this flake-gold is, that it can be found on high bluffs, just like down at the river; there is a little of it everywhere. Even if you go

INDIAN IN CANOE AND THICK VEGETATION, MCQUESTION RIVER

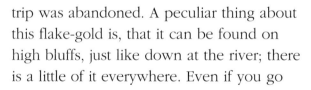

INDIAN CHILDREN ON THE MCQUESTION RIVER

THE MCQUESTION
RIVER

OUR BOAT GOING
THROUGH SWIFT
WATER ON THE
MCQUESTION RIVER

back from the river a mile or two and sink a hole 8 or 10 ft. deep, you can find the same colors in the soil there. We are now 680 miles inland from Dyea (at the coast) and 4,680 miles from New York.

July 18.

Not caring to waste any time up here, we floated down stream in our boat and arrived at the Indian village in the afternoon. It took just 4 days to pull the boat up stream 40 miles, while on the return trip, floating with the current, the distance was covered in less than a day. The constant handling of wet rope caused the fingers on both hands to split open and I suffered considerable pain.

July 19.

The provisions we had cached here were placed in the boat and after paying the Indians a farewell visit, we started down Stewart River, intending to locate on a gravel bar about 40 miles below, where we found the best colors on the up trip. While enroute we met the two parties who wanted to join us at Stewart R. last month. They had not met with any better success than any one else, but were going to stay over Winter. It rained most of the time and in the afternoon the regulation thunderstorm set in.

July 20.

We landed at the gravel bar today and went to work at once, fixing up the camp and carrying our provisions up from the boat. Two rockers were constructed with the boards we had carried along in the boat. The rockers were lined with a blanket, which was spread over the side and bottom, for the purpose of catching up the flake gold as it separated from the washed gravel. The rocker was constructed as follows. On top was a square box, with a tin bottom, which had a number of holes punched in it, so as to permit the dirt to flow through, when the gravel was washed. Under the box was a slide, over which the dirt and water must flow to the bottom of the rocker and then out at the end, as per diagram. One man carried over the gravel in a bucket, while the other washed it. The water was supplied from a ditch, direct from the river and the man manipulating the rocker dipped his water from the ditch at the same time.

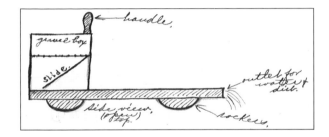

July 23-27.

Commenced washing gravel this day, working 8 hrs. The mosquitoes were fierce, but another, worse tormentor put in his appearance along about this time, in the shape of a tiny sand-fly, whose bite is worse than the sting of mosquitoes. This insect digs right down into the skin and nips off a bit of it. Mitt's were worn to protect our hands, while the face was shielded with mosquito netting sewed to the bands of our hats. On the following three days we worked 8 hrs. each day and on the 27th but half a day, because the result was not satisfactory. The gold was in the top layer of gravel and the deeper we dug down, the less gold was found. The net result of 8 hrs. work amounted to about $4.00 per man. This was the best bar along the river and we knew of no other locality to locate in. Not caring to remain here over Winter again, Geo. and I made up our minds to quit, return to the island below, sell out the balance of our provisions, etc. and sail back to the States. It was useless to go to Dawson City (only 70 miles below the mouth of Stewart) because at this time fully 10,000 people were roaming about the town with nothing in view and the ground all around the rich claims on Eldorado and Bonanza creeks, (Klondike District) was taken up long ago. It was a case of going out into new fields, looking for gold. Should we go below Dawson City into American territory, there would be no more hope of success than here and the Summer season is too short to accomplish much. Money and Cheatham (who by the way, owned the boat) wished to remain here a little longer and if not meeting with better success soon, would join us on the island. A raft was hastily built with 13 logs, having a sort of platform upon which to place our goods and fitted up with long sweep oars, fore and aft.

WASHING GRAVEL
WITH A ROCKER

WASHING GRAVEL
ON A BAR, OUR
ROCKER IN THE
FOREGROUND

OUR RAFT ON THE STEWART RIVER

Return to Seattle

July 28.

OUR GOODS WERE placed on the raft and after bidding our companions farewell, we started down the river at 2 P.M. The current was only moderate along here and since we wished to make as good time as possible, no stop was made. Our lunch was prepared and eaten on board, while enroute. We floated with the current in the main channel and worried about nothing. But the unexpected always happens. Late in the afternoon, we were floating down the right bank when suddenly we came to a narrow side channel, with a cross current. A little island was just ahead. Already the current was drawing us towards this side channel, which was swift water and full of rocks. But we worked our two sweep-oars so vigorously that we just managed to get back into the main channel and clear the point of the island ahead. A raft is an awkward thing to handle and had we gone down that side channel, it would have been wrecked on the rocks. The trip was continued until 7 P.M. when a big gravel bar afforded us favorable camping ground. It was very warm during the day, but the nights are always cool.

July 29.

This morning a thin sheet of ice was discovered on the water in our buckets. The sun sets at 10 p.m. and rises again several hours later. We left the bar at 7 o'cl. this morning and never stopped until we reached the island at the mouth of Stewart R. at 6:15 P.M. (Just 16 ¼ hrs. traveling 70 miles, on the raft.) Running the raft through the few swift currents encountered along this route was great sport and we managed to avoid accidents.

PREPARING LUNCH ON BOARD OUR RAFT WHILE TRAVELING DOWN THE STEWART RIVER

July 30.

A rough counter was fixed up in front of our camp and our goods displayed for sale— reserving enough food only for the trip out to the coast. It is our intention to travel on foot back up the Yukon and Lewis rivers and then to follow the Dalton Trail, (overland cattle trail) all the way out to the coast, total distance 500 miles. Beans, rice, corn and oatmeal sold at 10 cts. a lb. while sugar and fruits brought 25 cts.—we were anxious to dispose of the goods and did not haggle much over the price. Steamboats were running up as far as Five Fingers, but we made our minds to walk the entire distance, just for the novelty of it. Our destination was to be Pyramid Harbor, opp. Chilkat, on the Chilkat River. My partner Geo. had an attack of scurvy and I became alarmed lest he could not undertake the long journey out to the coast. It started with a swelling of the feet and legs and next day even his gums were found to be swollen. Geo. blamed it to the bacon, and I considered myself lucky in escaping the disease, for I had eaten three times the quantity of bacon and never felt better in my life.

Aug. 2.

To our surprise Money and Cheatham returned today. Money joined us and Cheatham went to Dawson City (70 miles).

Aug. 5.

Our last goods, including picks, shovels, pans, carpenter tools, etc. were sold today and Money also sold his outfit. A party of four, consisting of Wm. Packard, from Dixon, Ill., Money, Geo. and myself decided to travel together. Packard had a small boat, which came in handy for the trip up the river. Seven rolls of films which I had were packed up and mailed to my brother in Milwaukee. (They reached him one month after I got there myself.) Speaking about mail matter puts me in mind of a letter sent to me

from N.Y. and addressed to Dyea. We had already left Dyea, so it was forwarded to Lake Bennett and later on to Dawson City, but did not reach me. This same letter was returned and delivered to me in N.Y. six months after I had returned there. It traveled over 9,000 miles and all for two cents!

Aug. 6.

Our provisions were loaded into the boat and at noon the party started up the Yukon R. pulling the boat on a 75 ft. line. Geo. was permitted to do the steering, which gave him a chance to rest his swollen feet. The banks of the river were lined with brush and fallen trees, just as we found them along Stewart River. Our task was a hard one, but we are going back to civilization and the Dear Ones we left behind and the very thought of it gives us additional strength and endurance. We traveled just 6 hrs. today. Some wild cranberries were found along the river. These we cooked and gave to Geo. in the hope that the acid they contained would assist in checking the scurvy. This proved to be the case, for after several days, Geo.'s health had much improved.

Aug. 7.

White River was passed at 10 A.M. The weather was quite warm today, but we traveled 8 $3/4$ hrs.

Aug. 8.

This day was hot and we suffered considerable—traveled 10 hours. (The hours given is actual traveling time—I made a note of it every day, to show how long it takes to make the trip.) There is nothing of interest along here to write about.

Aug. 9.

Off again! Passed Tulare Creek at 10 A.M. and traveled 10 hrs.

Aug. 10.

Traveled 9 ³/₄ hours. Prospectors are camped along these creeks and rivers, but very little gold had been found. I had bought a new pair of rubber boots just before leaving Stewart R.—they came in handy on this trip, because of the daily wading that had to be done. But often we are walking over gravel and sharp rocks and rubber boots are not made for that kind of work. They wear out fast and become leaky—but for the time being, they render good service.

Aug. 11-14.

Passed Sellwyn (or Sullivan) Creek this day and traveled 9 ³/₄ hours—likewise on the 12th. The weather continues warm. We always take an early start, travel until noon and take a good rest during the hottest hours—then continue our journey until about 6 o'cl. The woods are full of berries, such as black currants, raspberries, high-bush cranberries, and the little round black goose-berries. Today we found this whole assortment within a space of 150 ft. square. I

must again mention the acres of wild roses, all in full bloom—a beautiful sight. We also found blue-berries, low-bush cranberries and huckle-berries, more than we could begin to pick. The bear up this country feeds on berries and fish, both of which are plentiful. Geo. is feeling much better now—he takes his turn at the rope the same as the rest. On the 13th we put in 10 hours and on the 14th, 7 hrs., arriving at Fort Selkirk at 5:30 P.M. (We covered 104 miles in 80 ¹/₄ hrs.) The evening was spent with the Police, Packard attending the little church at the further end of the village.

Aug. 15-17.

We disposed of some more provisions and clothing and left Fort at 2 P.M. bound for Five Finger Rapids (55 miles up Lewis River). The trail along the river bank was a poor one—thick brush was encountered and besides the current was a little swifter than in the Yukon. In many of the side channels the water was so low that we could not float our boat over the bars. All hands then waded out into the water and pushed the boat over the gravel and sand, into deeper water. It was very hard work, on account of the current. We traveled but 4 hrs. and were all very glad when the hour for rest came. On the 16th we kept at it for 9 ³/₄ hrs. and on the 17th 10 hrs. The boys are all very fond of pancakes, with cooked berries; so they are served every day. Traveling in the burning sun makes me feel so thirsty that I am longing for a glass of nice cool lager; but the only lager to be had is that which comes flowing down the mountains from the snow beds. One can drink that all day long—it will not quench the thirst. The country is more level along here, while along the Yukon high bluffs often obstruct further progress. At such places it was no easy task to get the boat around. Hugging the rocks closely, we would pull the boat by inches, simply by getting a grip on the rocks (often with our finger tips only). There is no chance to walk, for these bluffs generally run straight down into the water. Often, when with greatest care and effort we managed to reach the end of one of these bluffs, the current, which runs in shore and exerts its greatest pressure at this point, would catch the bow of our boat and force it around and down stream again. Then the whole work had to be gone over again.

Aug. 18.

Today we found loads of huckleberries and cranberries. They are rather tart, but when cooked and sweetened with sugar, they are very fine eating. Everything tastes good up in this country however and perhaps they are not quite as good as the berries we get at home. In the woods where it is a little damp, these berries (particularly huckleberries and the low-bush cranberries, which show just above the moss) are found in great numbers. In many places the moss (which grows a foot deep) is literally covered with them—a sight that would make the mouth of many an epicure water. Bear tracks were discovered at various times in the sand along the banks of the river, where

bruin was probably looking for fish. When Packard does the cooking, our pancakes are never well done—the rest of the boys like to have them crisp—and there is always a lot of kicking going on; but all in a good natured sort of way. We traveled but 4 hrs. today and camped 21 miles below Rink Rapids, where another big outfit, with cattle and horses had its headquarters. These parties had taken a lot of cattle inland over the Dalton Trail and rafted them to Dawson City, where fresh beef commanded a good price. A couple of good horses were just what we wanted to carry our provisions overland to the coast. We picked two good ones—a mare and a little sorrel horse and paid $80.00 for them, including pack-saddles and halters, complete. They were sold so cheap, because when Winter set in these poor animals would starve, for lack of food. The boat was sold for $10.00 to a couple of the boys, who wanted to take a trip to Dawson City.

Aug. 19.

Our provisions were packed on the horses and the trip continued along the high plateau, adjoining the river. From now on better time was made and we traveled just 7 hours, today.

Aug. 20.

The Rink Rapids were passed at 11 A.M. and we camped 2 miles below Five Finger Rapids, where the cattle trail leads across the river. We discovered two stray sheep in the woods and Money and Packard killed one of them, thus providing a good supply of fresh meat. These sheep had evidently swam ashore from some raft that was possibly wrecked on the rocks in the Rapids, or else they strayed away from some herd on shore. Fresh meat was a delicacy at this time—we had nothing but bacon and a little dried moose meat, which was given to us by some boys from La Crosse, Wis. at Stewart R. We traveled 6 hours today (covered 53 miles in 40 ³/₄ hrs.). A good mutton stew was prepared for supper—to the broth was added a little rice and dried potatoes and the boys said they would never want anything better to eat. It happened to be my turn at cooking and I had every reason to feel as proud as an old mammy down south. But when I asked them how they would like to enjoy a nice big piece of strawberry shortcake with cream, they appreciated the joke and I dare say their mouths watered. From this day on Packard and myself attended to the cooking, while Money and Hartmann looked after the horses. There is a little sawmill across the river and we appealed to the boys there to come over with a boat the next morning and assist us in crossing.

Aug. 21.

Bright and early this morning they did come across with a large boat and loaded up our provisions—the horses had to swim. Another party of three happened along at this time and each paid $1.00 for the use of the boat. One of the horses was held on a long line and the other on a shorter one, so they would not get tangled up in the water, which had a 12 mile [an hour] current at this point. With 6 men at the oars and two holding the horses, we started across this wide river and managed to reach the opp. bank ¹/₄ mile below. (The boat drifted this distance with the current.) Our mare sank under water twice, but was pulled along and landed safely. The little sorrel could swim like a fish and kept his head above the surface nicely. After landing, the horses were given a good rubbing down and allowed to rest. At 10 A.M. we were again under way, following the cattle trail, which was to lead us 350 miles overland out to the coast (Pyramid Harbor). The trail, which was very dusty winds its course over ridges and along many small lakes. We traveled 6 hrs. and camped in a woods, near a small lake.

Aug. 22.

Arose at 4:30 had breakfast and left this beautiful camping ground at 6:30. Half an hour later a little creek was waded at 9:30, we forded the Nordenskjold River. We are now 1 ¹/₂ miles from McCormick's Post (a landing place on Lewis R.) and 25 miles from Five Fingers. The creek is just 12 miles from the Fingers. Today's tramp lasted 8 ¹/₂ hours.

Aug. 23.

This day we hit a good trail, along which there was also plenty of feed for the horses. We traveled 9 hrs. and camped near a big lake. In the woods we discovered a fine patch of cranberries, where one could pick a hat full in a little while.

Aug. 24.

Left camp at 6:50, waded the Nordenskjold at 8:15 and again at 10 o'cl. (The river winds its way along the valley, while the trail takes a direct route.) 9 $\frac{1}{4}$ hrs. was the limit of today's tramp and we camped again near a lake. Often we see no trace of any water for miles, but we generally manage to find it before evening.

Aug. 25.

7:15 A.M. found us again on the move. The nearer we approached the coast, the more anxious we were to make good time; this is on the homestretch. Had our lunch on the bank of the Nordenskjold R. There were high mountains all around us—the scenery is fine. The trail is covered with a layer of fine dust 3 or 4 in. deep. The woods are full of grouse, but we have no time to hunt. Traveled 8 hrs. today and were pretty well tired out.

Aug. 26.

Our horses are in fair condition—only one of them is a little sore on the wethers, from the constant rubbing of the pack-saddle. These sores will wear a horse out quicker than anything else, so we are taking pretty good care of him. Left camp at 7:30, waded a river at 10:15 and then climbed a high ridge, passing from one valley into another. The trail runs along a high plateau, from

which an elegant view of the surrounding country is had; and then down a very steep grade, to the Indian village "Hoochei," which is about 100 miles from Five Fingers and 95 miles from Dalton's Post,* the next settlement. Dalton's Post is about 150 miles from the coast. Going down the steep grade we feared every minute the horses might fall down on top of us. The ground was a little wet and the poor horses could not get a foothold; they just slid down as best they could. Reached Hoochei at 12 n., had our lunch and immediately started out again for Dalton's Post, traveling 7 $\frac{1}{4}$ hours this day.

Aug. 27.

Off again at 7:10 and waded another river at 12:15. Twenty two miles from Hoochei we were forced to wade through a big swamp, where the horses came very near getting stuck in the mud. (We saw several dead horses sticking in mud up to their bellies and did not care to lose our faithful animals in that way, if it could be prevented.) In the worst places we spread branches over the soft mud before we dared take our horses over. After traveling 10 $\frac{1}{4}$ hrs. we reached Champlain Landing, on the Alsec River and camped there. Two of the Canadian N.W. Mounted Police, bound for Police Headquarters on the Klaheena River with 4 or 5 pack-horses, also camped here for the night.

Aug. 28.

The strain of this long journey was begin-

*Built by Jack Dalton, for whom the trail is also named.

ning to tell on our horses, so we gave them a half day's rest.

Last night it was quite cold and this morning the river was coated with a thin sheet of ice. Our little sorrel swam across the river during the night and was quietly feeding on the other side. We called and tried in every way to coax him back, but he would not come. It was then suggested that the mare be let out of his sight and perhaps he would follow. Sure enough—back he came with a rush, swimming the river without any trouble. We left camp at 12:30 and traveled only 3 ¼ hours. A number of swamps were again encountered—it was pretty hard on the horses.

Aug. 29.

Started out at 6:45 in chilly weather and crossed some more swamps during the day. The snow-covered peaks of the Coast Range are looming up in the distance—we are getting nearer home. This morning fresh bear tracks were discovered in the sand, close to our tent. It was now clear to us why the mare tore herself loose during the night and pawed the earth in a manner that caused Packard to wake up and then go out on a hunt for the animal, finally locating her some distance away, near the water. The very thought of that bear gave him the shivers, for he had no firearms with him at the time. The bear was probably following up a herd of cattle, bound for Dawson City, but Packard did not think so. We traveled 8 ½ hrs. this day and again camped at a lake. This whole country is nothing but mountains

lakes and rivers. Reading about Alaska, at home, one has an idea that it is a perfectly barren, dreary sort of country—that is not at all the case. The weather is fine and healthy, the woods are alive with birds, squirrels and larger game—berries and flowers are found in great quantities and there are any amount of wild ducks and fish in the lakes and rivers. To be sure it is a perfectly wild country, but the scenery is grand.

Aug. 30.

Broke camp at 6:30 and waded a deep river at 8:30. We came across two fellows who were trying to pull their horse out of a mud hole into which it had fallen during the night. With our aid, the poor animal was soon rescued from its living grave, but it could not stand up on its legs. Besides it had a big sore on the wethers, which made it unfit for further service. The boys realized this and ended its misery with a shot from our revolver. Then, taking the packs on their backs, they followed us, on their long and weary tramp to the coast. Our horses are now so accustomed to the water that we need never urge them to cross a stream. Often we are in the lead and wade to the opposite bank before the horses reach the stream. They need only be called by their names (Nellie or Frank) and both immediately follow. This afternoon we met a few Indians; the first since leaving Hoochei. It was fortunate that we carried a long rope with us, for it came in handy in crossing streams that were too wide and deep to wade. The rope was fastened to the halter and one of the party mounted the horse, holding on to the pack, while some one on shore held the end of the rope. The horse then carried its heavy burden across the river and was pulled back by the rope. Then the second man crossed over in the same way. Thus each horse made two trips and the whole outfit was landed on the opposite bank. It was very hard on the horses—especially in swift water and gravel bottom. Our mare had an attack of colic this afternoon, as we were coming over the narrow trail, on a high bank along Klakshu Lake. But for a few bushes alongside the trail, she would have rolled down the bank and perhaps into the water. The first thing to do was to try and cure the colic. Packard was the right man in the right place this time. He pulled out his old bandanna handkerchief and touched a match to it, just letting it burn slowly. This he held to the mare's nostrils, so she could breathe in the hot air. Under a cover of blankets she began to sweat and an hour later was barely able to stand on her legs; but she recovered sufficiently to be led to the end of the lake, where we found good camping ground. A creek 20 ft. wide carried the water from the lake, where our camp was located. Klakshu Lake, as we discovered, was the Indians' favorite fishing ground. A number of shacks were arranged on the opp. side of this creek, where they hang up the salmon to dry and then pack it back to their Winter homes. We were told that some of these Indians travel 75 or 100 miles to reach this lake. And little wonder—for it is literally alive with fine large salmon, which come up the creek to spawn in the

lake. We can see hundreds of fish jumping out of the water, all over this lake and there was a steady stream of them coming in from the creek. It was a sight that would make any sportsman's heart throb with joy. If we could only linger here for a time, what sport we could have! Today we were on the march just 8 ¾ hrs. Geo. shot a fine 20 lb. fish in the creek and then we had a feast. There are so many fish in this creek that one could shoot with eyes closed and be pretty certain of hitting a fish. This sounds like a fish story, but I have not begun to describe what it was like. I am wearing moccasins on this overland journey (boots and shoes are worn out long ago). The soles of my feet are hard as leather and this continual tramping does not affect me in the least.

Aug. 31.

Our mare was in a bad way this morning, but we could not linger here and at 8:25 the caravan of tramps was on the move again. (We looked, for all the world, like a lot of hoboes.) Last night there was a fresh fall of snow on the mountains—a gentle reminder that we must hurry, for the Coast Mts. must be crossed yet. But this morning it rained so hard and our mare was growing weaker—so we tramped along for only 2 ½ hrs. and then rested for the day, as it was feared the animal might break down completely.

Sept. 1.

Started out again at 7 o'cl., the mare having had a good rest and plenty of grass to feed on; so she felt much better. It was a bad trail along here—mud and rocks everywhere. At 12 o'cl. another Indian village was reached, at a lake. Only one old Indian with his squaw and another White man were found here. The other Indians were away on a hunting and fishing expedition. Our stock of bacon was running low, so we bought some dried salmon from the Indian (2 fish for $1.00). At 3 P.M. we arrived at Dalton's Post (95 miles, in 47 $^1\!/_2$ hrs.). There was a number of camps here and Dalton's was the only store, where supplies could be bought for 50 cts. a lb. We were informed that the clerk in this store was robbed of a considerable sum of money several days ago, by a party returning from the interior. Only 150 miles more to the coast! It seems but a short distance now. There was some talk of gold being discovered in a river near here, but we placed no faith in it, thinking that these reports were spread in the interest of the trading post. After a brief rest, we moved on, crossing the Alsec River on our horses. There were 5 different channels to wade— all swift water and quite deep. When crossing one of them, Geo.'s horse started down stream and he came very near being carried away by the current. The scurvy has now entirely disappeared, and he feels as well as any of the rest—thanks to the berries. We are gradually getting on higher ground now and the weather is still holding out nicely. The scenery is just grand— mountains ahead, and all around us. Our tent was again pitched near a big lake after a march of 7 $^3\!/_4$ hrs. When we get our tent

pitched, the supper is hastily prepared and all hands retire soon after.

Sept. 2.

Broke camp at 7 o'cl. We are now out on a stretch of open country, with mountains on all sides. Some distance ahead we see a long steady up grade. Grades do not bother us however, as we are pretty well hardened to the work—but the horses cannot travel so fast. Our mare is growing weaker and it is only a question of time when she will break down altogether. At 12 N. we had reached the top of a mountain and stopped at a small lake for lunch. This was above timber line and we gathered weeds to feed the fire. The horses have practically no feed—nothing but dry grass and weeds. We are at snow level on top of a barren mountain, with not a living thing in sight. It is the most dreary and desolate spot in all our travels. Back of us lies the valley we just left and on either side are high mountains. Just ahead are still higher ones and we cannot see where the trail leads to, but must simply follow it, up or down grades, as best we can. There is some attraction to life when you are surrounded by living beings, even if they be only little birds flitting about, but up here on this barren mountain one feels as if he were way out of the world. We are soon under way again, anxious to catch a glimpse of the timber, a little parch of grass—anything but this barren waste of ground. The beautiful scenery is the only reward for the weary hours passed up here. At 4 P.M. the Alsec R. was again crossed in 5 different channels. What a wonderful change takes place all of a sudden! Here we found some scrubby willows and the grouse are running to and fro between the bushes. The Canadian Police, who were left behind at Champlain Landing, caught up with us here and bagged some of the grouse. One of the fellows was a crack shot and never missed his aim. The days are growing shorter and it was nearly dark before we came to a creek, where a little feed was found for our tired out and hungry horses. We traveled 10 hrs. today and it was a hard days work.

Sept. 3.

Left camp at 7:30. For the first time, we had difficulty in finding the right trail. It was in a big meadow, from which half of dozen trails ran in all directions, finally merging into one wide path. This afternoon we waded a bog, half a mile long, where there was no chance for rest. The ground is soft and springy and one must keep on the move, for fear of getting stuck in the mud. It was pretty hard on our pack-horses, for at every step they would sink down a foot and we dared not let them stand still for even a moment. It is just 15 miles to the next timber—we are once more on higher ground. Another river was waded 5 or 6 times. From a high plateau an elegant view of the surrounding mountains and valleys is obtained. We passed a little patch of timber, but it [was] yet too early to camp, so the outfit moved on. The next good timber patch is 22 miles from here. Suddenly we came to a deep canyon. The trail leads us

down a very steep grade to a creek, which is crossed in two places and then we climb and climb, up another steep grade, to a big plateau. It is again a steady up grade. Looking back to the other plateau, a pack-train of horses was observed, coming over the trail. They look like miniature toy-horses from this distance. Already it is growing dark and still no water in sight. I never suffered so from thirst in all my life. Timber is a secondary consideration, if we can only get water. Our mare is getting so weak she must be pulled along. At last we came to a big creek, where our thirst is quenched. Then we crossed over this and camped on the high bank opposite. We are now on the Coast Range, away up in the clouds at an altitude of about 4000 ft. and near the three summits, which must be crossed. It is cold and damp up here and not a stick of wood in sight—nothing but scrubby willow bushes. Enough of the dry twigs were gathered to build a little fire. For the first time our tent was not pitched, because there were no poles to hold it up with. A drizzle, like rain, is falling, overspreading the whole mountain. We are all shivering with cold and can hardly talk. There was no elaborate spread tonight, as all of us are tired out and in a hurry to lie down and rest. We were under way 10 ½ hrs. this day. Our sleeping bags were spread out on the ground, 4 in a row and then we just slipped into them, clothes and all and covered up with the tent. If the mountain had toppled over that night, I don't think that would have woke me up; but I slept soundly every night. There was scarcely any feed for our poor horses and what weeds were found surely did not appease their hunger.

Sept. 4.

At 3:45 A.M. all were out again, so as to get an early start—we want to get away from the mountains. It was very cold this morning—no change from the same old drizzle of last night and we suffered considerably. By 6:30 the packs are again adjusted and our tired horses move along at a slow gait. Ever since the mare had that attack of colic, she lost in flesh and grew weaker from day to day. The first 2 summits were crossed and by noon the party reached what is called "Rainy Hollow," where a halt was made for lunch and the horses were given a chance to feed on the grass, which is plentiful here. ("Rainy Hollow" lies between the two last summits and derives its name from the fact that in this particular locality it rains almost continually.) Here we also found a little timber and fine big blue-berries are growing along the trail. The route covered this morning was up and down, all the way. Mud holes are found everywhere and our horses had a rough time of it. After lunch we began to climb the 3d summit, which is a long steady up grade. The sun was now shining brightly, in remarkable contrast to the nasty weather of this morning. Again we are on a wide plateau, with snow-covered mountains all around us. Nothing but scrubby willows, coarse white moss and a few weeds are found up here. Once in a while we catch a glimpse of the Klaheena R. valley. When that is reached, we will say farewell to the

Coast Mts. and Chilkat Pass. Our mare dropped in her tracks several times, from sheer exhaustion—but the horse is doing nicely. At 3:30 P.M. the steep grade was reached, and there below us we beheld the beautiful green valley, with the river winding its course, as far as the eye could see. What a different scene this is from the barren mountains we just crossed! Soon we will be back to the scene of our struggle last fall, with the oxen. There are yet a few mountains to be crossed, along Chilkat R., but they are trifling as compared with these big fellows. The grade is so steep, that it is unsafe to walk in front of a horse, for fear he might land on top of you. In just $1/2$ hrs. time the valley was reached, where our tent was pitched in the woods. Our hungry horses greedily devoured the juicy grass and we just enjoyed watching them fill up. This was such a delightful change from the past, that I was tempted to remain here for a week. Today's trip lasted 8 $3/4$ hrs.

Sept. 5.

We decided to move on and so at 7 o'cl. all was in readiness for the 50 mile tramp to the coast. Only 50 miles more! A mere trifle to us now. It was 8 o'cl. when we came to the recently established Canadian Police Post, where all parties coming from the interior must report and register their names and addresses. Then the journey was continued until 12 N., which is lunch time. At 1:15 we were again en route. The trail here leads us along the banks of the Klaheena R. Our horses, by mistake, were taken across a narrow creek, with very swift water. We had lost the trail for the second time and had to drive them back again. The proper trail, as we discovered, led directly across the bed of the river. Just then a pack-train was approaching us from the opposite bank and we waited to see where it crossed, then taking the same route. This river is divided into a dozen different channels, all of which were waded. The current runs about 10 miles an hour and the water is ice cold. A little further on, in a shallow stream, we caught 4 nice salmon, which were tied to the pack-saddles and carried along. The trail now led us over a mountain and we endeavored to cross same before night fall. Our mare however, was so wabbly on her legs, that we could not make good time and as a result were compelled to camp on the mountain. It was already dark and no water in sight. After unloading the packs and attending to our horses, Geo. and I went out in search of water and after skirmishing around for a half an hour, found a swamp on the mountain side and at the further end of it, a little pool of stagnant water. Two buckets full of this were carried back to camp and in a short time we had boiled some of our salmon; this constituted the supper. Our supply of sugar was running very low—all we allowed at a meal was $1/4$ spoonful, to each. Strange to say, everyone had a craving for something sweet. $9\frac{1}{4}$ hrs. was the extent of this days march.

Sept. 6.

Broke camp at 7:30 this morning and in less than half an hour the outfit had arrived at the valley, where it was intended to camp last night. Here we had about 4 miles of wading, in mud and water. There were swamps and many little streams, running in all directions. Next, the entire bed of the Klaheena R. was crossed again; possibly 10 or 12 channels, all told. After that we waded the Salmon River. We are fairly living in water today. The Salmon is not a wide river, but quite deep and swift water. Money, who was a nervy fellow, waded the river first, carrying the end of a rope over with him—Packard held the other end. Another party of 6 caught up with us here and all waded over together, holding on to the rope. Packard, a man of perhaps 45, came over last. He wound the rope around his hand several times before he ventured into the swift current and the boys all took a hand at the rope and pulled him over. I'll never forget the scared look he had on him, when half way across and waist deep in water, the current nearly carried his feet from under him. But he held on like grim death and was landed in safety. On one of the gravel bars along the Klaheena we saw the grave of an unfortunate traveler who lost his life here last July, in the swift current. A large heap of rocks denoted the burial place and a piece of board nailed to a stake bore his name and address and stated the cause of his death. We had 20 miles more to Dalton's Tollgate, which is 13 miles from Pyramid Harbor. Only 33 miles to go—we will surely cover that distance by tomorrow P.M. Our faithful mare was completely worn out and we realized she could not hold out much longer; so we ended her misery with a shot from the rifle. The horse seemed to realize what had occurred, for he grew restless, pawed the earth and whinnied for his mate in a pitiful manner. The pack-saddle was left behind and each of us carried a pack on his back. Every now and then the horse would turn in his tracks, stand still, as if to listen, and whinny for the mare. Only after repeated urging would he continue along the trail. He was still in good condition and always at the head of the procession. If he happened to get too much of a lead, he would face about and wait until the party caught up. The trail now leads over the mountains along Chilkat R., it is the new one, which Dalton constructed and for that reason he charges toll. The old trail runs along the mud flats of Chilkat River. Pretty soon we caught a glimpse of Klukwan, the Indian village, across the river to the left, where old foxy Co-to-wah (the Chief) lives. I was really anxious to see the fellow again, so I could give him the laugh over the meat bargain last fall. It is now one continuous see-saw of up and down grades, but we don't mind it a bit, for our labors will soon be at an end. At 4:30 I caught a glimpse of Chilkat, through an opening in the bluffs—but it was only for an instant, as we did not linger. Then it was the same ordinary trail again, winding its way through the timber. I have worn out 7 pair of moccasins since we left Five Fingers, in spite of the strips of canvas I wound around them for protection. We traveled 7 $\frac{1}{2}$ hrs. today and camped at a creek on the mountain. The other party is still with us and all are in good spirits—singing songs and relating one another's experiences. Packard and I amused

ourselves by rolling great rocks down the mountain side and watching them crash through the woods and finally landing in the river below. Packard had the laugh on him ever since he crossed the Salmon River, holding onto the rope—he did not care to cross any more streams after that and we don't blame him either.

Sept. 7-23.

6:30 A.M. and all is astir again. One shouts, "All aboard boys, this is our last day on the trail," and soon everybody is in line and on the march. For a little while the trail continues over the mountains—then suddenly it runs down to the flats along the river, where we had many channels to wade. Geo. had the good fortune of bagging a grouse and we had the bird for lunch. By 1 o'cl. the caravan was under way again—for the last time; we were now on the big mud flat, near the mouth of Chilkat River. Money and I were in the lead for some time. The end of our journey was so close at hand that we could not go along slowly, even if we tried. Suddenly we observed that the tide was coming in fast. There was no other route leading to Pyramid Harbor, so we shouted a warning to the others to hurry along. The pace was doubled, so as to enable us to reach the Harbor before the flat was flooded. The bank all along here is lined with huge rocks and a horse cannot travel there. Already the tide was up to the rocks—not long after it was a foot deep, then 2 ft. We walked over the rocks, while the horse picked his own path the best way he could, around the edge of the rocks. We were marching in double-quick time to get in ahead of the tide. The water was up to the horse's belly as we made the last turn around the rocks and found a path along the shore, which enabled us to reach Pyramid Harbor at 4 P.M. after a 7 1/2 hrs. march. We were just 32 days traveling 500 miles, counting stops and delays—an average of 15 5/8 miles per day. The longest days travel was 25 miles and the shortest 5 miles. The actual traveling time was 263 1/2 hours (about 11 days, of 24 hrs.)

After partaking of a hasty lunch on the beach, a boat was hired for crossing the 2 1/2 miles of river, to Chilkat. We had no opportunity to dispose of our horse for any consideration, as horses were very plentiful just about this time. Much as we regretted to part with the faithful animal, there was no other alternative but to turn him loose and he promptly wandered off into the woods. Camp outfit and sleeping-bags were also left behind, since we had no further use for them. Arriving at Chilkat, all hands paid the store-keepers a visit. As luck would have it, we met Co-to-wah, the Chief, in one of the stores—but he had nothing to say; simply glaring at us, while we sneered and turned away. Being informed that the steamer *Farallon* was due at the Mission this evening (Haines' Mission) our little remnant of the 2 ton outfit was packed over the hill to where the steamer could be sighted. At the Mission we met all of our old acquaintances of last year, including Rev. Warren, the missionary. The old Indian, "Schwatka," who said "Klondike, 2 1/2 month, I go," was

hired as a guide for some party going in over the Dalton Trail—we had met him about 200 miles inland leading a big herd of cattle over the trail. He had really spoken the truth last fall, only he started out later than 2 1/2 months.

It was a long wait at the Mission, for the *Farallon* did not turn into the harbor until after midnight. After dickering with the captain for a few minutes, the whole party including our fellow travelers, was taken aboard in a boat. Good old Capt. Roberts charged us only $15.00 each for the trip to Seattle. Once again we had a bed to sleep in and pretty fair food. How good the potatoes and fresh vegetables tasted! We had not tasted any in nine months and one learns to appreciate these things. It is now just a 1000 mile run and we will be back to the beloved States—God's own country. Arrived at Juneau at 10 A.M. and had 2 hrs. shore leave, which enabled us to take in the town. I wished to buy some fancy moccasins from an Indian for souvenirs, his price being $3.50 per pair. When asked how much he would take for a dozen pair, he answered "all same, three and a half a pair." And he wouldn't take a cent less, either, for no argument on my part could convince him that he should shade the price on a dozen lot. On the 9th. we arrived at Ft. Wrangell, A.M. and left again at noon. The weather was pleasant and warm—we enjoyed the trip immensely, but all were anxious to reach Seattle as soon as possible. Late in the afternoon a heavy fog set in. The steamer tied up at Ketchikan, 10 P.M. A large salmon cannery is located here and Indians are employed to clean and prepare the fish for the canning process. I took particular notice that when a fish was cut open and found to be faulty in any way whatever, it was at once dropped into a chute, to the water below. There were possibly several hundred discarded fish floating around in the water. At 11 P.M. we were again en route, passing St. Mary's Island during the night. For the two following days the fog held out and it also rained considerable. Nothing worthy of mention occurred on board ship and it was rather unpleasant and dangerous, in the foggy weather, especially when a strong tide is running. We took the same route as last year, between the islands and mainland.

The steamer reached Victoria B.C. at 10 P.M. on the 12th. Capt. Roberts and most of the passengers proceeded up town, for a few hours of recreation—but it was night and we could not see much of the town. At 2 A.M. everybody had returned to the boat and 15 minutes later the steamer was well under way. It was still very foggy, disagreeable weather. Port Townsend was the next stop, at 7 A.M. on the 13th. One and one half hrs. later we were off again, for our last port, arriving at Seattle about 12 o'cl. noon. No time was lost getting to a hotel and a good bath was the first item in the programme. My underclothing had not been changed since the beginning of August (for I had no other to put on) and it was as stiff as heavy canvas. The bath was quite refreshing. Next I had my year's growth of beard shaved off and my hair trimmed. The barber frowned when he saw what a big job he had on his hands and charged double rates.

Then Geo. and I went out to buy some respectable wearing apparel, for we looked like tramps with our leather coats, torn hats and shabby moccasins. Geo. and I separated here, he going to Tacoma. I spent 10 days in Seattle, undecided as to my next move. My wife had been in Europe during my absence, but had already returned to Chicago, where I was to meet her and our two boys.

I left here on the 23d and traveled to Chicago over the Northern Pacific, in company with P.J. Lawlor, of Indianapolis, who had also just returned from the Stewart R. region. My wife's first remark, after the hearty greeting, was, "How you look!" And I must confess she had good reason, for the rough life I led in Alaska had left its mark and I was not very particular in the selection of my clothing at Seattle. After a brief visit to the old home in Milwaukee, and a two week's rest at Chicago, I took my family back to New York, to enjoy life once more in a civilized community.

Since leaving New York, 14 months ago, I traveled about 1,750 miles on foot and the furthest point reached was up on McQuestion River, about 4,670 or 80 miles. The cost of the trip was about $1,000. While it was not a profitable one financially, I shall never regret the experience. It was of great benefit to my health (having gained 15 lbs. in weight) and that after all, is worth more than all the gold in Alaska. Now that the trip is at an end, all seems like a dream to me. I would not hesitate to make the same trip again, providing I had something profitable to look forward to. It is a fine country—all it needs is transportation facilities and better development. There is lots of gold there—also silver, copper, iron and coal, but it will take years before it can be mined on a paying basis (excluding gold) and be put into our markets. What we missed more than anything else, in that northern country, was the entire absence of news of any sort. While up there we were indeed lost to the World.

Place Names

The names at the left are place names the way William Shape noted them in his journal. The spellings at the right are the more commonplace versions.

Alsec (river): Alsek

Cariboo (crossing): Another variation frequently seen is Caribou Crossing.

Chilcoot (pass): Chilkoot

Douglas (island): Douglass. The name is actually spelled both ways, although Douglass is the most accepted form.

Hootalingua (river): Hootalinqua

Klakshu (lake): Klukshu

La Barge (lake): The name has a variety of spellings, also including Labarge and Leberge. The latter is the most common.

Lewis (river): Lewes. Properly, this river has always been the Lewes, named for John Lee Lewes, a chief trading factor for the Hudson's Bay Company. Shape, along with others over the years, simply misspelled it.

Lindemann (lake): Lindeman is the generally accepted version today; the lake name had a variety of spellings during the gold rush, including Linderman, in addition to the above two.

McQuestion (river): This was a misspelling on Shape's part. The river (and a river settlement) has always properly been spelled McQuesten, named for Leroy (Jack) McQuesten, Yukon trader and founder of Fort Reliance and Circle.

Skaguay (city): Skagway

Stikeen (route and river): Stikine

White Horse (rapids): Whitehorse

Yindistucka (village): There are many variations on this name. The most common "Y" spelling is Yindastuki. The correct geographical name is Gantegastaki.